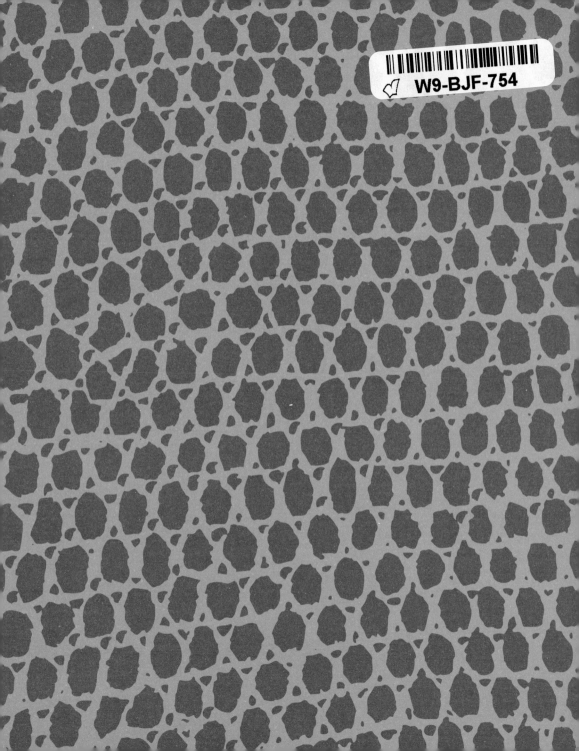

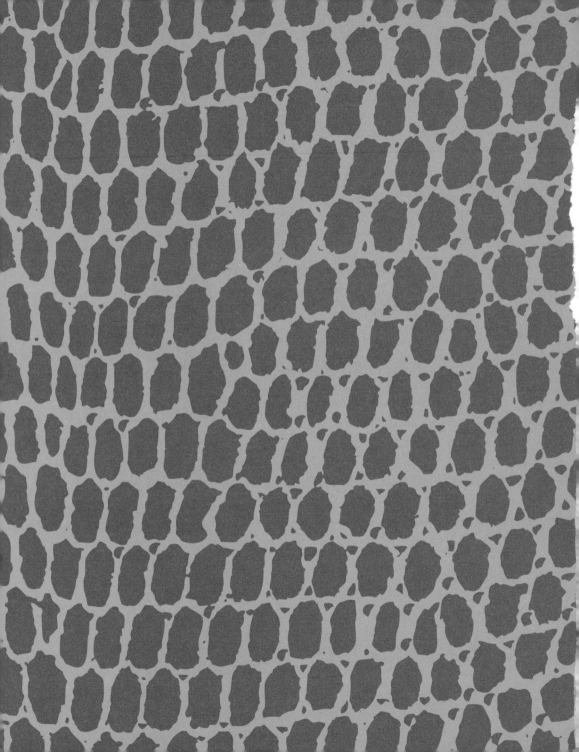

Setup and Care of
Freshwater
Aquariums

DAVID E. BORUCHOWITZ

Freshwater Aquariums

Project Team
Editor: Brian M. Scott
Copy Editor: Mary Connell
Series Design: Stephanie Krautheim & Leah Lococo Ltd.
Design: Angela Stanford

T.F.H. Publications
President/CEO: Glen S. Axelrod
Executive Vice President: Mark E. Johnson
Publisher: Christopher T. Reggio
Production Manager: Kathy Bontz

T.F.H. Publications, Inc.
One TFH Plaza
Third and Union Avenues
Neptune City, NJ 07753

Discovery Communications, Inc. Book Development Team
Marjorie Kaplan, President and General Manager, Animal Planet Media
Patrick Gates, President, Discovery Commerce
Elizabeth Bakacs, Vice President, Creative and Merchandising
Sue Perez-Jackson, Director, Licensing
Bridget Stoyko, Designer

Printed and bound in Indonesia.
09 10 11 12 13   3 5 7 9 8 6 4
ISBN 13 978-0-7938-3760-1

Library of Congress Cataloging-in-Publication Data

Boruchowitz, David E.
  Setup & care of freshwater aquariums / David E. Boruchowitz.
     p. cm.
  ISBN 0-7938-3760-X
  1. Aquariums. 2. Aquarium fishes. I. Title. II. Title: Setup and care of freshwater aquariums.
  SF457.3.B59 2006
  639.34–dc22
  2006012103

The Leader in Responsible Animal Care for Over 50 Years!®
www.tfh.com

Table of Contents

Introduction

Setting up a freshwater aquarium is not a difficult project—with one provision. You have to know what you are doing. You cannot simply fill a tank with water and dump in some fish. That is a perfect recipe for disaster. The expert tips in this book, on the other hand, will guide you to set up your first aquarium successfully.

Many undertakings require special knowledge that is not self-evident; in fact, sometimes the correct procedure might seem counterintuitive. For example, it is not hard to bake a chiffon cake, but if all someone has is access to a kitchen, he or she will not be able to create one. Even given all the ingredients, it is unlikely that an inexperienced cook will succeed.

Similarly, driving a car with a manual transmission is extremely easy…if you already know how. Even skilled drivers will be unable to succeed if they lack experience or instruction with handling a clutch and knowledge of how the transmission operates.

An oversimplified analogy would be a situation in which you receive various sets of directions to get from New York City to San Francisco. Following any one of them will get you to your goal, but if you divided up all the instructions and took the first few steps of one, then the next steps of another, and so on, you would become hopelessly lost.

Think of this book as a cookbook or a roadmap that will teach you how to set up an aquarium that will become a habitat for a thriving fish community for your enjoyment. The path delineated here will get you safely to that goal. Other paths will as well, but the simple steps outlined here will get you there safely. Once you are a successful aquarist, you can learn more advanced techniques and grow in the hobby.

The Goal

The assumed goal of this book is that you will be able to successfully create a freshwater community aquarium—a tank that will contain a variety of peaceful fish. These types of fish are by far the most common selection new aquarists choose for their first aquarium. The basics, however, are the same for any type of aquarium that you might want to set up.

So, relax, read, and then go on to set up your first aquarium!

Chapter 1

Why Do YOU Want an

Aquarium?

You certainly have seen aquariums, perhaps in a doctor's office, a restaurant, or someone's home. Maybe you enjoy browsing through the aisles of a pet shop, looking at all the tanks of fish for sale. And now you've decided to set up an aquarium of your own. Congratulations!

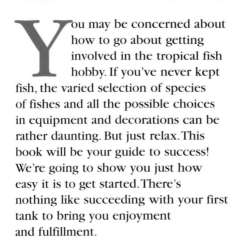

You may be concerned about how to go about getting involved in the tropical fish hobby. If you've never kept fish, the varied selection of species of fishes and all the possible choices in equipment and decorations can be rather daunting. But just relax. This book will be your guide to success! We're going to show you just how easy it is to get started. There's nothing like succeeding with your first tank to bring you enjoyment and fulfillment.

Aesthetics

People maintain aquariums in their homes for many reasons. The first has to be the beauty of a nicely set up fish tank. An aquarium is like a living picture—fish of different shapes, sizes, and colors move dynamically through the tank, which may also house living plants that float in the current and add color and texture to the work of art. Unlike elements in a static picture, colors and shapes in an aquarium are always changing, making it a kaleidoscope of natural beauty. The

Armchair Vacations

How would you like to take a trip to an exotic tropical locale whenever you felt like it? Well, an aquarium in your home can transport you to faraway places. With just a little imagination, watching your fish for half an hour can refresh and enliven you.

characteristic behaviors of the fish also add interest.

Many aquarists forget this aesthetic aspect—how important the beauty of an aquarium was in attracting them to the hobby in the first place. Although they started with an aquarium meant to decorate their home, they became so interested that they began to specialize; they tended to keep certain types of fish, or breed particular species, or even went on to enter their prize specimens in fish shows. Their many aquariums often fill whole fishrooms and none of them are decorative in nature.

A single specimen of a large species can make a fascinating display.

The fish alone motivate them to continue in the hobby.

On the other hand, some aquarists become so enthralled with decorative aquariums that they fill their homes with one after the other, perhaps neglecting the aesthetic value of a varied community of interesting fish.

Relaxation

Have you ever wondered why you see so many aquariums in doctor's waiting rooms, in schools, and in restaurant displays? They are not so common in banks, supermarkets, or gas stations. The reason is that watching fish is relaxing. In places where people gather and have to wait, an aquarium often provides a focal point, something they can watch while they wait.

Even persons who just pass by typically stop for a moment to watch the fish. Children, especially, are unlikely to pass an aquarium without stopping for a look. That's why they aren't popular in places where people are supposed to keep moving rather than loitering.

In fact, some aquariums are used therapeutically. They are set up in patient areas because it has

The Expert Knows

Something for Everyone

There are more than 20,000 species of fish in the world, and at least 2,000 are routinely available in the tropical fish trade. They range from tiny fish less than an inch (2.5 cm) long to 50-foot (15-m) behemoths. There are fish that live on land, fish that lay their eggs on leaves overhanging water, fish that go to sleep in the mud when their pond dries up—while they wait for the rainy season, and many, many more.

So, even if you have decided to become an aquarist for some other reason, you are still sure to benefit from the peaceful pastime of watching your fish. You might even find yourself turning more often to your aquarium than to your television set!

Natural Beauty

Many people enjoy the beauties of Nature. They like to surround themselves with living things, especially in response to the increasing artificiality of the world around us. A few generations ago, plants and animals were part of almost everyone's daily life, but today most people live and work in high-tech

been known that watching an aquarium reduces anxiety and stress. Even the sound of running water from the aquarium's filtration system has a soothing effect. Now you will be able to reap the same psychological and emotional benefits from a fish tank that patients in hospitals and nursing homes enjoy.

Actually maintaining an aquarium, rather than just observing one, can also have positive benefits. Children learn responsibility and compassion when they realize that other living things depend on them. Persons who are lonely and infirm often find solace and a renewed sense of dignity by caring for animals; that's because people feel useful and appreciated when their pets depend on their assistance to survive.

A Benign Addiction

Many aquarists define their hobby as an "addiction," and the passion they have for their fish can certainly seem extreme. Fortunately, the aquarium hobby is constructive and educational, and while not really addictive, it often provides a lifetime of enjoyment and a feeling of accomplishment.

environments filled with inanimate objects. An aquarium is like a garden— a little slice of nature brought into someone's home, as a way to reconnect with nature and the diversity of life on our planet.

Aquariums offer virtually limitless possibilities to sample this natural bounty. Some people take a collective approach during their travels; they find and bring together plants and animals from all over the globe, choosing them by idiosyncratic criteria—whatever especially appeals to them.

Others try to replicate natural habitats. They set up a tank to resemble a particular habitat somewhere in the world, choosing plants and animals that would be found together in that locale. Still others are drawn by different features and behaviors of the fish themselves. They might enjoy keeping large predatory fish, or colorful schooling fish, or even "oddball" fish—fish that swim upside down, for example, or species that navigate via electric fields.

There are so many possibilities, but let's take a more detailed look at these three common approaches.

"Here, Look at This One!"

The aquarium of an idiosyncratic collector serves as a home to various fish—each intriguing the collector for some reason. He or she is always eager to point out the features of various fish and explain what makes each species interesting or unique. The collection may be quite unique and it serves the aquarist as a constant reminder of the miraculous diversity of living things. The theme of this type of tank is simply the sum of all the characteristics of its fish inhabitants.

Such a setup can be very rewarding, but it can also cause a lot of problems. Not all fish get along well, and sometimes one species prefers conditions that are stressful to another. In later chapters you will learn what you need to know in order to avoid such problems, so that if you want to start this type of collection, you will be able to succeed with it.

"It's Just Like a Stream in Borneo!"

An aquarium that mimics a specific natural habitat can be very educational as well as ornamental. Many public aquariums have a series of tanks, each representing the type of plants and animals that might be found in different places around the world. Such tanks express a theme of an exotic locale, reproducing some tropical ecosystem in miniature.

A home aquarium can be a more modest version of these displays. If this type of collection appeals to you, this book will offer you the basic information you need to get started

SMALL FRY

A Child's Tank

Even very young children enjoy watching an aquarium. Long before children are able to care for some fish on their own, they can learn a great deal just by having their own tank. Encouraging them to "help" maintain the aquarium will teach them responsibility, compassion, and a respect for living things.

in this direction. You might have to consult other books to find out just which fish and plants can be found in the particular habitat you select, but at least you will already know how to

The Siamese flying fox is one of the many interesting Asian fishes.

Special Tanks

One interesting type of fish collection focuses on an aquatic theme that features a certain trait or group of traits of the fishes. This is less common as a first aquarium, since you would have to know something about the fish to come up with a preferred set of traits in the first place. Why not just choose fancy guppies with different colors as the only inhabitants of the tank, or make up another tank using only different species of tetras.

select and care for them based on what you have learned here.

Are You An Accidental Aquarist?

I use this term to describe persons who either receive an aquarium as a gift or inherit it from someone who no longer wants it nor is able to maintain it. These accidental aquarists often become some of the most dedicated lovers of aquariums.

If that is your case, then this book should prove especially useful to you, since you are coming to this hobby without having decided for yourself that you want to! You are forced to learn what to do and may have no previous experience of even observing an aquarium. You're starting with a completely blank slate.

No matter what has brought you to consider starting an aquarium, sit back, relax, and read through this book. By the time you have finished its contents, you'll have the information you need to begin a successful foray into the fascinating world of tropical fish.

Chapter 2

The Stuff You
Need

A trip down the aisles of any aquarium store will demonstrate that an enormous amount of equipment—and assorted goodies to go along with that equipment—is available, enough, in fact, to be overwhelming. Fortunately, the equipment you *need* to set up a successful aquarium makes up only a small fraction of all that is available. This chapter outlines the basics to help you cut through the confusion.

Aquariums

Obviously, the first thing you need for your project is the aquarium itself. You must first decide the size and shape you want, and then you can choose between glass and acrylic plastic.

Size

Aquariums are available in standard sizes from 2.5 gallons (9.5 l) to 265 gallons (1,000 l), and in just about any size you wish in custom-designed models. There are many factors to consider in making this choice, but all choices are not equal. Obviously you have to take your available space into account and the type of fish you want to keep, but it is important to buy the biggest tank that will fit into your plans.

The major concern in maintaining an aquarium is dealing with the waste products of the fish, many of which are quite toxic. A larger volume of water is more forgiving of mistakes in management. Thus, a larger tank will remain more stable despite your lack of experience.

Another reason to choose the largest possible aquarium is that you can keep a wider variety of fish. A very common mistake fledgling aquarists make is to overstock an aquarium in their enthusiastic attempt to include all the most interesting species. A larger tank allows more leeway in stocking. The minimum I'd recommend for your first tank is 20 to 30 gallons (100 l). The popular 29-gallon (110-l) tank is good— even better is the 55-gallon (209-l).

Shape

To an extent, the shape you choose for your aquarium is a matter of taste. It's important to take the surface area of the water in relation to its volume into account. This has to do with gas

Weighty Matters

Don't underestimate the weight of an aquarium! Figure on approximately 10 pounds (5 kg) for every gallon. This takes into account the weight of the tank, gravel, and water. A 55-gallon (210-l) tank, therefore, weighs in at about a quarter ton (227 kg)!

Why? Well, consider the different effect produced by pouring a small amount of a toxic substance into a 5-gallon (19-l) bucket of water compared to a 5-acre pond. If there were fish in both, the ones in the bucket would be much more likely to suffer injury or death, simply due to the much lower rate of dilution.

exchange—getting oxygen into the water and carbon dioxide out. Thus, squat, wide tanks provide more gas exchange than tall, narrow tanks having the same volume. Powerful water movement, which effectively increases the surface area of the water, can handle this concern.

A few extreme tank shapes, —tall cylinders or tall square prisms, for example, cannot be properly aerated and it is very difficult to perform maintenance on them. Spherical aquariums are best used half full; this maximizes the surface area, which otherwise might be as small as the surface area of a canning jar.

Another consideration is the footprint of the tank—the size and shape of its bottom. In almost all aquariums this is the same size as the surface area, but what we are concerned about here is the amount of area to provide fish territory rather than gas exchange. Some fish are territorial, and almost all territorial fishes stake out a territory on the

bottom. A tank with relatively more volume than footprint will have less room for territories than a squatter tank of the same volume. This will have

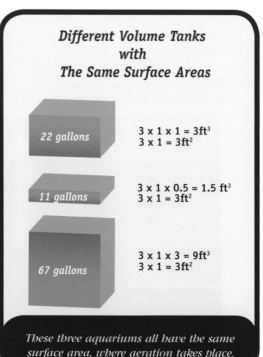

Different Volume Tanks with The Same Surface Areas

22 gallons
$3 \times 1 \times 1 = 3ft^3$
$3 \times 1 = 3ft^2$

11 gallons
$3 \times 1 \times 0.5 = 1.5 \ ft^3$
$3 \times 1 = 3ft^2$

67 gallons
$3 \times 1 \times 3 = 9ft^3$
$3 \times 1 = 3ft^2$

These three aquariums all have the same surface area, where aeration takes place.

serious consequences with some species and be of little concern with others.

Glass or Plastic?

Glass and plastic tanks have different properties, so you should make your choice according to which type of tank best fits your needs. Acrylic plastic aquariums are very popular, especially with marine hobbyists who keep saltwater fish and invertebrates.

Plastic tanks are very durable. It takes more of an impact to break plastic than glass, so an acrylic tank is less likely to crack if something bangs into it. Plastic also is a better insulator than glass, so an acrylic tank loses heat more slowly than a glass one, providing a more stable environment for your fish and leading to slightly lower electric bills for you.

Although plastic is harder to crack, it's more prone to being scratched than glass—carelessly scraping algae

Not One Way

There isn't a single way to set up or maintain an aquarium. That's part of what makes it confusing for the new aquarist who gets different advice from everyone. This book is dedicated to cutting through all the confusion and presenting a simple, straightforward recipe for success with your first aquarium.

from the front panel can ruin a plastic tank with unsightly scratches. At the same time, acrylic is optically clear, meaning that it's colorless no matter how thick it is. Glass, on the other hand, has a greenish tint, though this is usually only a concern in very large tanks with thick panels. Fortunately, types of glasses containing low iron are available and aquariums constructed from them are quite clear.

Glass or Acrylic

	Glass	Acrylic
Pros	Costs less. Harder to scratch.	Lighter. Break resistant. Optically clear. Retains heat well.
Cons	Heavier. Easy to break. Has a greenish tint. Loses heat readily.	Costs more. Scratches easily.

Two final parameters are important to consider when you first set out to acquire your first tank—acrylic tanks are more expensive than glass tanks of comparable size, which makes them harder on your budget. On the other hand, glass tanks are considerably heavier than acrylic, which makes them harder on your back.

The table to the left summarizes the pros and the cons of each type of aquarium. Glass is usually the better choice for a first tank, but you can certainly succeed with an acrylic one.

A custom-made stand and canopy can add beauty to any aquarium.

Stands & Canopies

The stand on which your aquarium sits can be as simple a construction as two-by-fours on cinder blocks or as elaborate as a hand-carved hardwood cabinet. It must be designed to be absolutely sturdy enough to bear the weight of the tank full of water. Many modern aquarium stands are beautiful pieces of furniture; it is simply not safe to use furniture that was not designed for the purpose. A nightstand is designed to hold a lamp and a phone, not several hundred pounds of water!

Likewise, the cover for your aquarium can be as simple as a sheet of glass with an aquarium-type light strip on it or as elaborate as a full-fledged canopy that matches a hand-carved hardwood cabinet below and houses high-tech lighting strips and cooling fans. The primary function of the aquarium cover is to keep the fish in the tank—any fish can jump, and many species are especially prone to jumping out of the tank.

If you want to maintain live plants in your tank, you will need to choose adequate lighting for them to grow. If you are not going to have live plants, then choose whatever lighting you like best, as your fish will probably not care.

The water movement caused by an airstone is much more important than the actual air bubbles themselves.

Filtration & Aeration

The familiar bubbling aquarium ornament is passé. You do not need air bubbling into your aquarium. If you like the look of bubbles rising in the tank, you can use an air pump with a wide variety of ornaments, or you can use an air-driven filter that releases bubbles.

On the other hand, if you don't need the bubbles, neither do your fish. Gas exchange takes place at the surface—the interface between the water and the air. An air bubble is a very small surface, and it rises very quickly and escapes, so not much gas exchange takes place via the bubble. Even a whole lot of bubbles still effect very little in the way of direct gas exchange. Bubbles do, however, make the water move, and that is very beneficial.

Most power-driven filters provide even more water movement than bubblers do. Establishing a moving current in the aquarium effectively causes the water surface to be constantly renewed. The more water movement there is, the more gas exchange—aeration—takes place.

Filtration is necessary for your aquarium; if someone tells you it is not, do not believe them. In fact, your chance of success with your fish tank is greatly increased if you have the proper filtration. So since you will be using a filter, it will provide aeration, making bubbles unnecessary.

People speak about three types of filtration, and they are all based on this simple principle: water from the aquarium passes through any of the media, which in some way purifies the water, and then the water returns to the aquarium. Specific characteristics of the individual types of media determine how filtration is accomplished. Many aquarium filter devices combine more than one type of filtration.

Mechanical

Mechanical filter media trap suspended particles. This is what most people think of as a true filter—like a coffee filter. Slots, holes, or fibers create spaces that are smaller than dirt suspended in the water, so it is trapped as the water passes through.

Such filtration clarifies the aquarium's water. In fact, it is possible to use micron filters like diatomaceous earth units that will remove even single-celled organisms from the water—the so-called "water polishing." The tank water continues to pass over the medium, however, so any decomposition of the particles that takes place while they are still trapped in the filter continues to pollute the tank until you remove the medium and either clean it or replace it.

Chemical

Many substances dissolve in aquarium water. Since they become dissolved at the molecular level, they cannot be filtered out by a regular mechanical filter. Instead, chemical media are used. Specific chemical substances target other specific chemicals—zeolite for ammonia, certain resins for phosphates, etc.—but the most common chemical medium is activated carbon. High temperatures and pressure cause this carbon to become extremely porous at the molecular level, and many chemical molecules are drawn into these micropores. The process is called *adsorption* because

the carbon pulls the chemicals into itself. Depending on the exact nature of the carbon and the size of its micropores, various dissolved substances will be attracted and grabbed.

The benefits of chemical filtration is most important in systems with complex chemical balances, such as marine reef tanks. It works well in any aquarium, however, its importance is often overemphasized. This is because simple water changes do more for your aquarium than carbon filtration ever can, since water changes remove many more dissolved substances than carbon can. In other words, there is nothing wrong with using activated carbon in your filter, but you should not rely on it to keep your water pure.

Biological

Biofiltration, by far the most important type of filtration, is named because the purification of the water is performed not by the

Canister filters have the ability to provide mechanical, biological, and chemical filtration.

21

biomedium in the biofilter, but by bacterial cultures that live in the medium. That's right, bacteria. Those microscopic little workhorses make the difference between life and death for our aquarium fishes.

The concern here is the waste materials the fish create, which consist primarily of ammonia. Ammonia is extremely toxic in the environment for fish, and even small amounts can burn the delicate tissues of a fish's gills and fins. Slightly greater amounts will kill a fish outright. But fish are constantly producing ammonia!

In the wild, this is rarely a problem, since enormous volumes of water immediately dilute any ammonia and take it elsewhere in the body of water in which the fishes live. The equivalent in a captive number of fish would be something like a dozen 2-inch (5-cm) fish producing ammonia in a swimming-pool-size aquarium that also had a fresh water stream flowing constantly into the tank and overflowing out the other end. But a typical aquarium is nothing like that, which is why we need filtration

in the first place, and biofiltration especially. Two kinds of bacteria are needed for bio-filtration, but fortunately they both have the same requirements: space to grow, food, and oxygen.

Surface Area

The biomedium provides the place to grow. Surface area is what's important here, since these bacteria don't like to float around in the water, and they can't function properly if they are all piled up on top of each other. Obviously, then, a substance full of microscopic nooks and crannies would be ideal. Of course bacteria will grow on surfaces like the glass panes of the tank, but a piece of glass 12 inches (30 cm) by 24 inches (60 cm) has only 288 square inches of area, a mere 2 square feet (1,800 cm^2). By contrast, a pound of activated carbon—with all its microscopic pores—typically has a

Porous rocks, like these lava chips, provide a lot of surface area for biofiltration.

total surface area of 125 *acres* (309 hectares) or 5.45 million square feet (0.5 million square meters)!

Foam sponge is quite high in total surface area, and many biofilters employ a sponge medium. Sponge is easily cleaned; pollutants are removed simply by squeezing the sponge several times in a bucket of aquarium water. Aquarium water should be used so that the bacteria are not killed by the chlorine in fresh tap water.

This diagram illustrates all three stages of filtration.

Dirty Water from Tank
Fiber Medium (Mechanical)

Solids Out
Carbon Medium (Chemical)

O_2 Impurities Out O_2

NH_3 and NO_2 to NO_3
Sponge Medium (Biological)

Clean Water to Tank

Food

The first type of biofiltration bacteria feed on ammonia, which is certainly good news for aquarists. Unfortunately, they produce nitrite as waste. Nitrite is toxic to fish, and though less toxic than ammonia, it can quickly kill when concentrations reach only a bit higher than the lethal level for ammonia. But there's more good news!

The second type of biofiltration bacteria feed on nitrite. They produce relatively benign nitrate as waste. Nitrate isn't good for fish either, but it can build up to considerable levels before it really starts to harm them. Regular water changes will remove the accumulated nitrate—as well as other pollutants—since they are by far the most important factor in successfully maintaining an aquarium.

Oxygen

Biofilter bacteria are aerobic, that is, they only live in oxygen-rich environments. Unfortunately, water can only contain a certain amount of dissolved oxygen, depending on the water's salinity and temperature. At best, this averages around 6 to 8 ppm. Air, on the other hand, is oxygen rich with about 200,000 ppm.

Many biofilters rely on a constant supply of oxygenated water flowing over the biomedium to supply the bacterial colonies with oxygen, and this works quite well. Other filters, however, try to exploit the fact that air contains about 20,000 times as much oxygen as water. Biofilter bacteria can only live in water, but, being microscopic, they don't require very deep water. In fact, a slight film of water is all they need.

The Stuff You Need

Wet-dry technology takes advantage of this. Several modern filter designs include a wet-dry component, which greatly increases their usefulness. A high-surface-area medium is kept wet, but exposed to air. Some wet-dry filters trickle or spray the water over a porous material, while others use a pleated fabric wheel that rotates into and out of the water just like an old-fashioned water wheel. The result is a great deal of wet surface area that is separated from air only by a very thin film of water. Since oxygen dissolves very quickly into a water surface, and in a wet-dry filter basically all the water is surface, plenty of oxygen is available for the bacteria.

This increase in available oxygen translates into increased biofiltration capacity, so a certain amount of medium in a wet-dry setup will provide a great deal more biofiltration than the same medium would in a flow-through setup.

Types of Filters

A great many filter designs are available today; all of them are good and designed to aerate and filter the tank water well. Making the best choice is very often a matter of personal taste. For the beginner, efficiency and ease of use are important, and for this reason I recommend a power filter

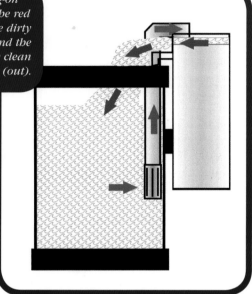

A typical hang-on style power filter. The red arrows indicate dirty water (in) and the blue arrows show clean water (out).

that hangs on the outside of the tank. Most of these have modular media in cartridge form. They are easy to change and do not require you to handle the filter medium directly. They have only one moving part and do not require hoses or valves, making them simple to operate and to clean. An impeller pulls water from the tank and sends it through medium-containing compartments, after which it exits back into the aquarium via an overflow.

Usually there is a choice of media, with mechanical, chemical, and biological filtration possibilities. The modular nature of many models enables you to mix and match media to fit your system the best.

There are certainly many other types of filters that will work for your first tank, but our suggestion for a first tank is a hang-on power filter. In terms of efficiency, economy, and ease of use, you will definitely do well with a hang-on power filter.

Because they hang on the back, these filters are unobtrusive, and the only part that is in the aquarium is the siphon tube, which is easily hidden by aquascaping. It is also a simple matter to remove the filter for cleaning or servicing without disrupting the tank. Several manufacturers make filters of this design, and there are many different features available. These filters are typically available in a range of sizes, rated in gallons per hour (gph). This indicates the maximum flow rate through the filter, and you should look for one whose flow rate per hour is between six and ten times the volume of your aquarium.

Heaters

Unless you live in a tropical climate, your house probably gets too cold, at least part of the year, for most tropical fish species; they are most comfortable in the 76° to 80°F (25° to 28°C) range.

To maintain that range in temperature, you'll need to acquire an aquarium heater. The most common aquarium heaters are the hang-on and submersible types. Both consist of a tube, usually glass, with a heating element and a thermostatic switch inside. Most can be adjusted to the precise temperature you wish to maintain. Follow the manufacturer's instructions for the original calibration, and then adjust to your precise needs with the help of an aquarium thermometer.

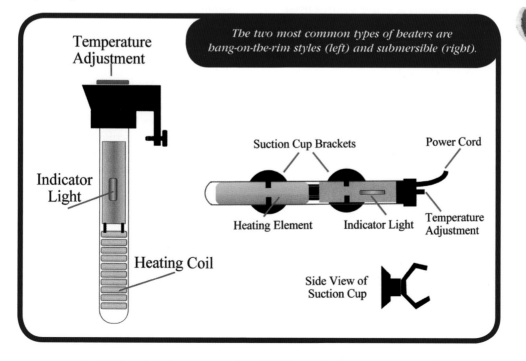

The two most common types of heaters are hang-on-the-rim styles (left) and submersible (right).

Temperature Adjustment

Indicator Light

Heating Coil

Suction Cup Brackets

Power Cord

Heating Element

Indicator Light

Temperature Adjustment

Side View of Suction Cup

Aquascaping is often easier to do when the tank is only partially filled with water.

Heaters are rated in watts (W), with most models available in sizes from 50W up to 300W. Since large volumes of water gain and lose heat much more slowly than small volumes, the larger an aquarium, the smaller the relative heater it needs. So, for example, a 20-gallon (76-l) tank usually needs a 100W heater, but a 60-gallon (227-l) tank, three times the size, needs only about a 200W heater.

Of course, the room in which the aquarium is located also comes into play. If it experiences unusually low temperatures, or wide temperature swings during the day, then a larger heater will be needed than if the room is warm and stable.

You are generally okay if you figure 5 watts-per-gallon (3.8 l) for smaller tanks and 3 watts-per-gallon

(3.8 l) for larger ones. When in doubt, slightly larger is the better choice, since an uncustomary drop in room temperature can overwhelm an already maxed-out heater.

Substrate & Decorations

Coarse sand or fine gravel are the typical substrates in home aquariums. Although many fish enjoy digging in the substrate—and some actually bury into it, almost no fish commonly kept in aquariums actually require it. In fact, many breeding tanks are kept bare-bottomed, since this facilitates cleaning.

Nevertheless, most people like gravel in their tanks, and an enormous assortment of suitable products is available, in both natural shades and vivid colors. The only thing to avoid is gravel with sharp or rough edges,

Neon Gravel & Bubbling Divers

Children often want an aquarium that would appear garish to an adult. The way a tank is decorated reflects the aesthetics of the aquarist. To the fish, it's basically all the same, so let a child's imagination soar.

such as crushed glass and large pebbles. Glass can injure fish as they pick around for morsels of food, and large spaces between pebbles can trap uneaten food—or even small fish! A fine or medium gravel is best, while sand can cause problems.

Decorations serve two functions: aesthetics for you and hiding places for your fish. Some fish are cave dwellers and basically come out only to feed, but almost any fish will be more comfortable if there is a handy cave or bunch of plants into which to dash if it feels threatened.

Various types of rocks and driftwood are popular ornaments, but you should buy items specifically produced for the aquarium to avoid contaminating your tank with undesirable substances that could leach out of the

rocks or wood. Plastic plants, which look almost like the real thing, are also very popular.

A vast variety of ceramic, plastic, and resin decorations are available, with something for anyone's tastes. Miniature fairyland villages, realistic imitations of human skulls, shipwrecks, toxic waste barrels, and "No Fishing" signs are among the hundreds of choices. Many of these feature cavities in which timid fish can hole up.

Live Plants

Live aquatic plants make a beautiful addition to an aquarium, but they are by no means necessary. Some fish eat them, and most like to hide out in them. It is an easy matter to provide vegetable-based fish foods in the absence of plant material, and plastic plants and other ornaments serve fish as well as live plants in providing hiding places and a sense of security.

Living plants have specific needs, many of which are not the same as fish's needs. This means that a planted tank, in the

Plastic ornaments can look very realistic, like this piece of "driftwood."

sense of an aquatic garden, puts a primary focus on the plants, while the fish become secondary elements—almost ornaments.

Live aquatic plants are available in a wide variety of shapes and colors.

On the other hand, you can easily include a few live plants in your tank without getting involved in all the special equipment and concerns of aquatic gardening. Since lighting is the most important concern for plants, those plants that can survive under regular aquarium lighting are very popular. Java fern and various species of anubias are perfect choices. Not only do these plants do well with minimal light, they also prefer not to be planted in the substrate. They will grow attached to rocks or driftwood, or even with their rhizome sitting on top of the gravel.

Test Kits

Many test kits can provide valuable information to hobbyists about the chemical nature of their tap water and of the water in their tanks. When you are first starting out, however, you should make a few crucial tests, and leave the rest for some future time

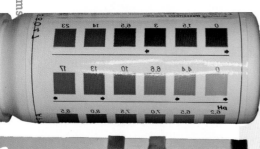

Today's test kits allow the hobbyist to perform multiple tests at one time.

when you are involved in maintaining rare species or breeding finicky ones. Your local dealer can tell you if your water supply is so extreme that you cannot keep common aquarium fishes; otherwise, I recommend not getting hung up on all the chemistry as many people do. However, if you want to keep a few types of test kits handy, then those that test for ammonia, nitrite, and nitrate would be the best ones.

pH & Hardness? No Worries!

Specifically, I recommend that you ignore concerns about the hardness and pH of your water. They simply aren't that important for achieving your goal of a successful community aquarium set up for beauty and enjoyment. I realize I am bucking a lot of "expert advice" by saying this, but I have observed more useless worry and fussing by new aquarists about pH and hardness than about any other topic. Sometimes the efforts of the aquarist to deal with perceived problems actually wind up harming or killing the fish. The simple truth is that the vast majority of aquarium fish will do fine in the vast majority of public water supplies. The new aquarist who is not concerned with breeding fish or keeping rare, expensive species simply does not have to worry about water hardness and pH.

This is definitely an area where a little knowledge is dangerous, and even many veteran aquarists do not completely understand the ionic chemistry of water solutions being bandied-about in terms like pH, hardness, alkalinity, conductivity, salinity, etc. Do yourself a favor and ignore these things for now.

Methods of Cycling

Last, but very far from least, you need to choose a method of cycling your tank. The notion of aquarium cycling has reached quasi-mystical status among many aquarists, who, often armed with very little chemical knowledge, expand and expound on the subject until it seems the

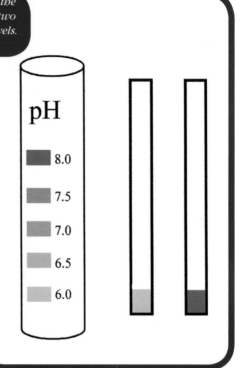

The strips at the right indicate two different pH levels.

procedure is almost beyond human abilities. There really is a simple way of cycling your tank, however.

Actually, there are two simple ways, but first we need to define what we're talking about. "Cycling" is a bit of a misnomer. There is a natural process referred to as the Nitrogen Cycle. Here is a simplified version of it: nitrogen gas from the air is fixed by soil bacteria, taken up by plants, and converted into proteins. The plants either die or are eaten by animals. The animals excrete wastes such as ammonia and eventually die. Decomposition of plant and animal material also produces ammonia. Certain bacteria feed on ammonia and produce

Platies are hardy fish that can survive the cycling process.

nitrite as waste. Other bacteria feed on nitrite and produce nitrate as waste. Still other bacteria feed on nitrate and produce nitrogen gas as waste, which goes back into the atmosphere, completing one round of the cycle.

That was the simple version? Yes, but you don't need to worry about it. The "cycle" aquarists talk about is much simpler, and technically it isn't even a cycle. You probably noticed that in that the process described earlier as biofiltration is a good description of the Nitrogen Cycle. Well, that's what cycling is: getting a biofilter going.

This means you must have a source of ammonia, which will get the first type of bacteria started. You will know they are on the job when ammonia levels start to drop and nitrite levels start to rise. Once ammonia goes to zero, nitrite should be falling and nitrate should start

accumulating. There are two easy ways of maintaining the cycle.

Patience!

Remember that cycling your tank can take more than a month—depending on the method used. This is time well spent, however, since there is nothing more important to a new aquarium than a properly functioning biofilter. All you need will be your test kits and plenty of patience.

Method 1

The traditional cycling method is to start with a few very hardy fish like zebra danios or platies. The fish produce ammonia, beginning the cycle. Daily testing will alert you to any dangerous buildup of ammonia or of nitrite, in which case a partial water change will often bring the tank right back into the safe zone. When ammonia and nitrite test consistently zero, you can add the rest of the fish, a few at a time, until the tank is fully stocked and maintaining zero levels of ammonia and nitrite. Add a few fish, then test the water daily until levels are back to zero. (It is possible with a strong biofilter to add fish and not get any measurable ammonia or nitrite buildups, in which case you can add more fish in a day or so.) Repeat the process until you've put in all the fish.

This process can take up to six weeks, though it can be less. The reason it is popular is that it works, and it gives you at least a few fish in the tank. So-called "fishless" cycling goes much more quickly, but there aren't any fish in the tank until the biofilter has matured. If you have that kind of patience, there is an even easier way to do this.

Method 2

Since cycling a tank means maturing a biofilter, you can get a biofilter going on one tank and then just move it to your tank. This requires, of course, a friend or a willing retailer to help you out. Take the filter you will be using and install it on an established aquarium, such as friend's or neighbor's tank. A slightly crowded tank is best; your filter will help alleviate extra stress on that tank, and the heavy bioload will help mature the new biofilter. Leave the filter running for four to six weeks. Then bring it home and set it up on your aquarium. You should add about half the fish you plan for the tank. Wait a few days, testing for ammonia and nitrite every day. If they remain at zero, you can add the rest of the fish. Continue water testing every day or two to be sure the biofilter is up to the challenge. If you do get a spike of ammonia or nitrite, a partial water change will fix things.

The Expert Knows

Truly Necessary Tests

The absolutely mandatory tests you need to perform are not on your tap water, but on the water in your tank, and they are needed to track the process of cycling, which we'll cover next. You have to be able to test for the three biofiltration waste products: ammonia, nitrite, and nitrate. You need to be able to perform these three tests, though some kits enable you to test for more than one at a time.

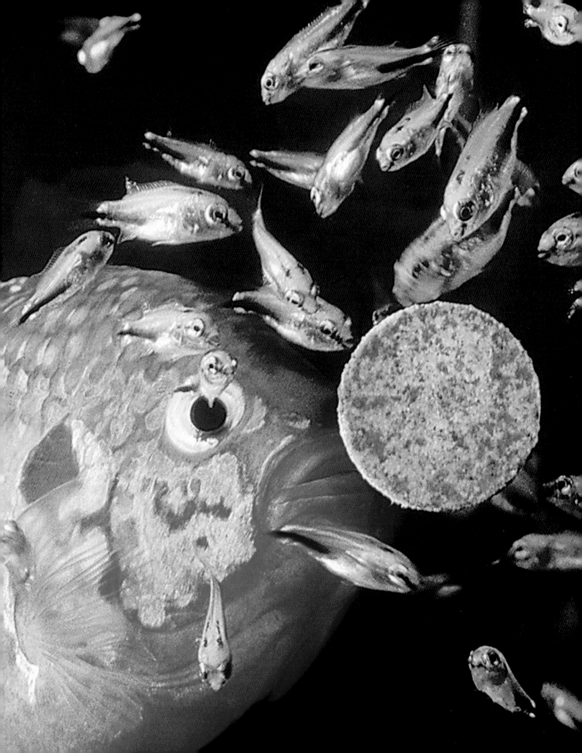

Chapter 3

Good Eating

One of the easiest things to do in caring for your fish is feeding them, yet new hobbyists often make many mistakes in this area. Why? Well, as I've said, it isn't because of the difficulty of the task, rather it's due to a lack of understanding. When we feed a pet cat or dog, we can relate to the process, but fish are cold-blooded, and, unlike a pet lizard or turtle you might have cared for, fish do not bask in warm areas to digest their food. This means that we really have no frame of reference against which to measure our fish's eating habits. Before we tackle this problem, however, let's take a look at the kinds of foods you'll be dealing with.

Commercial Foods

Fish foods are made in a staggering variety, with each manufacturer producing many different foods. They can all be divided into three groups: dry, frozen, and freeze dried.

Dry Foods

These products differ in ingredients, of course, but they also exist in various forms. Flake foods are made by rolling the ingredient mixture into an extremely thin sheet and drying it to form a less-than-paper-thin sheet. This is then broken up into little bits or flakes that are fed to the fish. For very tiny fish, the flakes can be further crushed, or even rubbed between thumb and forefinger into a fine powder.

Flakes are available in different formulations for herbivorous, carnivorous, or omnivorous fishes, and in formulations based on different main ingredients such as eggs, brine shrimp, or earthworms. They are fortified with vitamins and minerals. Usually there is a mixture of flakes designed to float, sink slowly, and sink quickly; this gives surface, midwater, and bottom feeders equal chances to get their meal.

About the only drawback to flake foods is that they are simply too meager for large fish. Any fish over 4 inches (10 cm) or so is unlikely to be able to eat enough flake food to sustain it properly, but even foot-long (30 cm) specimens will often greedily suck in these obviously tasty foods, and they make a good vitamin-rich treat for them now and then.

Pellets & Sticks

When the formulation is extruded rather than rolled into sheets, pellets or sticks are produced. While sticks are strictly for large fish, pellets are available in a range of sizes from tiny bits small enough for many

Spice Things Up

Feeding a wide variety of foods keeps things interesting for your fish, as well as providing more complete nutrition. The majority of fish like to pick at things, taking a nibble here, a nibble there. Providing flake, frozen, and freeze-dried offerings will help satisfy your fish's need to exploit different types of foods.

newly hatched fry all the way up to hearty lumps perfect for feeding the biggest specimens.

Wafers

There are many wafer foods on the market as well. The ingredients are pressed or molded into disks which sink to the bottom when dropped into the tank. One of the most popular varieties is the algae wafer, made out of *Spirulina* algae, sometimes mixed with other ingredients. These are ideal for herbivorous catfish, which feed primarily on the bottom. Since these fish are nocturnal, the wafers are dropped into the tank after the lights are turned off at night so that the catfish will get their fair share.

Frozen Foods

Originally frozen foods were a substitute for live foods, and they were simply food organisms flash frozen to preserve nutrients. Commonly available were frozen brine shrimp (both baby and adult), *Daphnia* or water fleas

(a small freshwater crustacean), and bloodworms (actually the larvae of an insect).

Today, however, a great variety of additional frozen offerings are available, including combinations of food organisms and blends of all sorts of foods. There are even special frozen preparations for marine fish that feed on live sponges.

Frozen foods are typically received by aquarium fish with the same enthusiasm that live foods elicit, and they are nutritious

Many fishes react to frozen foods with the same gusto as if they were live foods.

Many types of freeze-dried foods can be pressed against the glass so you can easily watch the fish feed on them.

Freeze Dried Foods

Freeze drying is a process in which water is removed under low pressure and low temperature—a method that preserves much of the original nutrition and palatability of food organisms. The resulting product is light, dry, and crumbly. Although it doesn't look or feel like much, this type of food has an enormous appeal to fish. Apparently the flavor and odor is preserved, and the feeding response these foods elicit is remarkable.

Specialty Foods

Many innovative foods on the market are produced for very specific needs. For example, there are pellets formulated and sized specifically for bettas. They are packaged in a container that doubles as a feeder, enabling you to feed one pellet at a time.

treats for your pets.

Obviously frozen foods must be kept in the freezer. You should never refreeze them. To use, simply break off a piece the size you need and drop it into the tank. There is no need to thaw the food; the fish will start picking on it, and as the warm water thaws the food, they will be able to eat it.

Some people don't like the fact that when the food is frozen, the organisms' cells burst, letting some of the nutrition flow into the juice surrounding the individual food animals. They feel that since the fish do not consume this liquid, they are missing part of the food value. This is certainly true, but as with human frozen foods, a quality product is prepared in such a way as to minimize this loss. Budget brands often have less nutrition than more reputable products.

Feeding time!

There are special wafers for bottom-feeding herbivores and for bottom-feeding carnivores. There are formulations for the specific dietary needs of different types of cichlids, guppies, livebearers, angelfish, discus, etc. All of these fish can do well on a general formulation, but some aquarists prefer to use foods specifically created for their favorite species.

Noncommercial Foods

You can easily keep fish healthy for many years using only commercially prepared and marketed fish foods. Nevertheless, there are other options for home processed foods.

Homemade

The era of homemade fish foods is past, yet some people still prefer to make their own foods. Usually these are made by putting various ingredients in a blender with a binding agent like gelatin and freezing the resultant paste or gelled food. This process is beyond the scope of this book, however. If you reach the point where you want to try this, you can consult other texts or the Internet for recipes and instructions.

Live Foods

Live foods may be purchased, but they are generally not commercially marketed for obvious reasons. Live foods of all types have enormous appeal to most fishes, and they are necessary to get some species conditioned for spawning. Foods that are widely cultured at home by aquarists include white worms, Grindal worms, baby brine shrimp, wingless fruit flies, daphnia, vinegar eels, and microworms. Starter

Many angel-fish breeders prefer to make their own homemade foods.

cultures are available from a variety of sources, especially from other aquarists, and they typically come with instructions.

Foods that are more often purchased than cultured include blackworms, tubifex worms, bloodworms, and adult brine shrimp. These can be purchased in portions from many aquarium stores, but sometimes aquarists get together and buy them in bulk to divide among themselves.

Fish Treats

The best treat for any fish is a swimming or wriggling critter about the size of the fish's mouth. Live food tempts a fish like nothing else. Even though live foods are not necessary for a fish's nutrition, it will greatly appreciate at least an occasional treat of a food like daphnia, brine shrimp, or blackworms.

Overfeeding

Overfeeding is without doubt one of the most common and most dangerous things that new aquarists do. The practice destroys a tank in many ways. Overfed fish produce much more waste than they normally would, and the food that goes uneaten falls into cracks and crevices, where it rots. It does not take long for putrefaction to set in, making the tank a stinking, septic mess. Long before that, the fish begin to suffer from accumulated poisons, and no biofilter can keep up with the ammonia produced. And, as with humans, overfeeding leads to

obesity in fish, which can cause serious medical problems.

Your goal as a new aquarist should be to underfeed, to err on the side of caution. If you are afraid of overfeeding your fish, good!

How Much To Feed?

I've never witnessed a new aquarist starving his or her fish, but I have known a great many who overfed them. When you overfeed your fish, you also overfeed your tank, pushing the bioload higher and higher until a crisis occurs.

The much-cited "rule" to feed your fish as much as they can eat in five minutes is setting you up to fail. Why? First, if you knew how much they could eat in five minutes, you wouldn't need advice on how much to feed!

Also, five minutes is a very long time. There are a few slow-feeding species of fish, but most are the feeding-frenzy type—they attack their food voraciously, trying to get it all before their tankmates do. Their bellies are bulging long before five minutes pass.

In addition, fish do not know when to stop. It is very rare for fish in the wild to find so much food at one time in one place that they can overeat. Hence, they do not have reliable mechanisms to limit feeding; rather, they are programmed to eat as much as they can whenever they can. This serves them well in the wild, but in captivity it leads to all sorts of problems.

A Better Strategy

A better way of learning to feed your fish properly is to figure out how much food your fish need to eat, instead of how much they *can* eat. Begin by counting out flakes or pellets of food, one for each fish in your tank. Take a look at that pile; it won't amount to much. No, you're not going to do this every time you feed your fish, but the amount you visualize this time will get you used to what the right amount of food looks like.

Then dump the food into your aquarium, and watch the fish. Did every fish get something to eat? Do they seem satisfied, with bellies slightly bulging? Probably not, but the food undoubtedly disappeared instantly.

Now do it again, and watch carefully. Repeat this at most one more time. Believe it or not, that was plenty of food for your fish. It may not have been the most they would eat, but it was a good start.

As fish reach satiation, they will show less interest in food. As long as none of your fish are frenziedly

Special care should be given when feeding aquariums that contain many fishes. Remember, all of them have to eat!

searching for food, they've gotten enough to eat. You will soon learn the appropriate amount to feed, and in the meantime you won't be overfeeding, but you have to make a conscious effort to underfeed at first.

Feeding Problems

Once you've learned how much to feed and how often, what other problems might you encounter?

Improper Diet

The nutritional needs of many pet animals are well known. Specifically formulated diets for various types of dogs and cats are based on copious research, but determining the exact needs of one or two canine and feline species is nowhere near the task that researching the nutritional

Don't Be a Pushover

Some fish are very good at begging for food. They can peer through the glass with soulful eyes and dance excitely when you approach. Don't fall victim to their persuasions.

Suckermouth catfish are popular algae grazers but they need some meaty foods in their diet to stay healthy.

wholesome and can be part of your pets' diet. However, other foods, even favorite foods, can undermine your fish's health in the same way that French fries and chocolate can be harmful to your dog. So, given that we don't know much about the nutritional needs of the thousands of fish species, what can we do? Well, fortunately, we do know quite a bit about what fish eat in the wild, and we know what foods have given good results in the aquarium, so

requirements of thousands of fish species is. Many fish are specialized feeders: some eat algae, others eat invertebrates; some eat other fish, others eat aquatic plants; some eat sponges, others eat mollusks, and so on.

In addition, even fish that have quite specific food choices in the wild acquire quite catholic food tastes in the aquarium, consuming items they would never get in their natural habitat. They can even prefer such foods, in the same way that most cats love cow's milk and tuna—two foods they will never encounter in the wild. And, like milk and tuna for your cat, many unnatural foods for your fish are

SMALL FRY

Lock up the Food

Putting your fish food under lock and key may be a bit extreme, but it must be kept away from children. Children have no concept of how much to feed fish. You can certainly have your child help you feed the fish, but never leave it so that the child can feed the fish on his or her own. Give the child the correct amount of food in the cap or on a piece of cardboard, and let him or her put it into the tank. This will help teach the right amount of food to give.

a simple method almost guarantees our fish will be properly fed: feed as wide a variety of foods as possible. This way your fish will get so many different nutrients that their exact needs will likely be met. Something that is lacking in one food is probably found in some other food. By eating a bit of this and a bit of that, your fish will get everything they need for good health, growth, and color.

Hunger Strikes

It is rare for a fish to refuse food, but it does happen. This can be a symptom of disease, but, unfortunately, by the time a fish is ill enough to stop eating, it is not likely to recover no matter what treatment you give it. There are, however, other reasons a fish may say no thanks to dinner. In these cases often what we see is a reduced feeding response: the fishes do eat, but not very enthusiastically.

One reason for this behavior can be temperature. If fish are too warm or too cold, their feeding can slow down or cease altogether. Obviously, this is one condition that is easily checked and corrected.

Another possibility is that the fish aren't that hungry. You may have been feeding too much, or perhaps there was a birth or a spawning in the tank, and all the fish are full of the fry or the eggs they gobbled up.

The Eye-Stomach Connection

The adage says that a glutton's eyes are bigger than his stomach, but a useful rule of thumb is that a fish's stomach is about the size of its eye. Like all rules of thumb, this one is limited in usefulness, but it certainly serves to get us thinking in the right order of magnitude—fish stomachs are *tiny*. If you are uncertain as to the amount of food to offer your fish, always err on the side of caution and feed a little less. Overfeeding is very dangerous, and aside from causing your fish to gain excess weight the overfeeding of your aquarium may cause the delicate balance of it to become upset—perhaps with devastating effects.

Fish sometimes get bored of the same old food and show a decreased feeding response. Switching to a new food will wake them up, and using a variety of foods on a regular basis will keep them interested.

Then we must factor in the above-mentioned cold-bloodedness of fish. After a two-week fast, fish are merely hungry; most warm-blooded animals would be dead or severely debilitated. Many predatory fish normally eat a large meal and then fast for several days to a week before eating again.

Keeping It All
Running

Once your aquarium is up and running, you will
need to spend some regular time maintaining
it. The requirement is modest, but the ease with
which you can take care of an aquarium should not
make you complacent. Regular maintenance is vital
to the well-being of your pets.

The most important thing you will do is to observe your fish. Spend some time just watching the tank. You will learn how your fish normally look and behave, and you will gain an intuitive sense that will alert you when something is out of kilter.

Water Changes

No maintenance is more important than regular water changes. Should these be performed daily, weekly, or monthly? Well, regular, partial water changes will do more to keep your fish healthy and happy than anything else you could do. Of course, good filtration and the wise use of the proper additives will assist you in keeping a healthy aquarium but nothing can really take the place of water changes when it comes to maintaining a clean and healthy environment for your fish.

Whenever water changes are discussed, two questions emerge: *How much?* and *How often?* The answer to both is: *The more, the better*.

Think of a toilet. An unflushed toilet. That is basically what an aquarium is. Your fish are constantly producing wastes. Besides urine and feces, fish also excrete wastes—mostly ammonia—through their gills. Unfortunately, they also breathe through their gills, drawing all those dissolved wastes across delicate tissues in an effort to take in oxygen and get rid of carbon dioxide.

An aquarium filter provides a short-term solution. It removes the most toxic substances and replaces them will less toxic ones, but many of the dissolved substances simply accumulate. The reason that aquarium water becomes yellow over time is that urine and other wastes build up until they are visible. Long before that, however, they are stressing your fish and causing their environment to degrade.

Pudding Proof

There are no fish that do not benefit from large, frequent water changes, and almost all will demonstrate with their health, color, and vigor that they greatly appreciate them. Those of us who promote very large, very frequent water changes do so because we have seen the results.

Many commercial breeders, especially of difficult-to-breed species, use regimens of 100 percent daily water changes—or even 100 percent *twice daily* water changes. In these extreme cases, no filtration is needed; the aquarium

Frequent partial water changes are a must!

water is always fresh and clean. Nothing encourages rapid growth of healthy fry like massive water changes, especially since the heavy feeding often used on growing fish will otherwise quickly overwhelm the system with pollution.

The idea is to keep that toilet flushed. By flushing huge quantities of fresh water through your aquarium, you guarantee that your fish have a stable, clean environment at all times. Pollution simply does not have the time to build up between water changes, and neither do all the other processes that can change the chemistry of aquarium water.

The Numbers Game

Although you will see recommendations of as little as 10 percent every other week, such water changes are barely better than nothing. It is probably easiest to visualize this in terms of total gallons of fresh water.

Consider a 20-gallon (76-l) tank. With the 10-percent biweekly regimen, in a month the fish in the tank get 24 gallons (91 l) of clean, unpolluted water (20 gallons [76 l] initially, 2 gallons [6 l] at two weeks, 2 more gallons [6 l] at four weeks). Raise that to 10 percent weekly, and the total is 28 gallons (106 l) in a month.

But if you change to 50 percent weekly, the number jumps to 50 gallons (189 l) of fresh water in a month! That represents 50 gallons (189 l) of water into which wastes can dissolve, twice the amount the fish receive under the first regimen.

Supplies to Keep on Hand

Your aquarium maintenance supplies should include:
- New filter media or cartridges.
- Water change equipment.
- Algae scrapers.
- A few plastic buckets used only for the aquarium.

Now consider that breeding operation where fry are being raised in 20-gallon (76-l) tanks with daily complete water changes. In this case, the fish see 20 gallons (76 l) of fresh water per day, 140 gallons (530 l) per week, and almost 600 (2,270 l) gallons of fresh water per month! It is little wonder that with such a procedure fish can be raised in aquariums that are comparable or superior to those raised in outdoor ponds.

You may ask if such is really necessary for a simple home aquarium. It probably isn't, but the closer you come to such maintenance, the better your fish will do and the more positive experience you'll have with your aquarium. Remember that your fish will produce the same amount of wastes in a specified period of time, no matter how much or how little clean water you provide them. The more clean water, the greater the dilution of the wastes, and the less clean water, the less dilution. A 50-percent weekly change seems to work very well for many people, and it is quite possible that after you see the water clarity and the exuberant response of your wet pets after each change, you will increase even that regimen.

The Procedure

Water changing can be simple or elaborate. The time-honored bucket and hose still work very well. Water-driven changers are quite popular and eliminate the possibility of spilling a bucket of water on the floor. These use the flow of water from your tap to create suction in a length of tubing. They will even pull water uphill, though not very quickly. When the desired amount of water has been removed from the aquarium, you flick a switch and the water flows from the tap back through the tubing into the aquarium.

The major drawback of these devices is that they waste a great deal of water—the water used to power the siphon pump. Many people use the pump only to start the siphon and then turn off the water and let the siphon drain into the sink.

As long as your aquarium is higher than a nearby drain (sink, toilet, or even a window leading to the garden), you can use a plain length of tubing to siphon water from the tank to the drain. A regular garden hose attached to hot and cold faucets can be used to refill the tank. You should always replace water with water of the same temperature to prevent shocking your fish.

All municipal water supplies and many wells are sanitized with chlorine or chloramine. These chemicals, which keep water safe to drink, are harmful to fish. Chlorine can be removed by vigorous agitation, but chloramine cannot. You should add a treatment designed to neutralize these sanitizing chemicals as you add the new water to your aquarium.

Daily Maintenance

Every day you will need to make brief contact with your aquarium. You will be feeding your fish, of course, but at the same time you will want to make several quick checks. Soon you will be performing these tasks almost instinctively.

Check the Temperature

Check the thermometer to make sure your heater is functioning properly. Do not constantly adjust the temperature, since no heater can keep the water at a precise temperature. Variations of a degree or two are not a problem. It is also a good idea to get in the habit of touching the tank with the back of your hand (your palm is not as sensitive) whenever you walk by it.

This will alert you to severe problems, such as the heater failing, in which case the glass will feel unusually cold, or the heater being stuck in the on position, in which case the glass will feel unusually warm.

Inspect the Filter

Is it working? Is the volume of the output undiminished? I have some filters that have been operating non-stop without a problem for a decade, but sometimes an impeller will get clogged, or a hose pinched, or a tube skewed out of its socket. When the flow of water through the filter is

SMALL FRY

Observation & Preventive Maintenance—a Good Job for a Child

Children are obsessively observant; they miss practically nothing. Enlist your children in keeping an eye on the aquarium and have them report to you whenever they detect anything amiss. Besides being an early warning system, you will find your children notice many interesting things about your fish, helping you to stop and smell the roses.

compromised or blocked, the filter ceases to function properly, and your fish are put at risk.

Look at Your Fish

Watch them. Get to know them. Aside from being one of the most enjoyable parts of this hobby, observing your fish will teach you how they normally look and act. This way, you will be alerted to any changes in their appearance and behavior that could indicate a problem.

Weekly Maintenance

All of the chores listed in this section can be performed more often than weekly, but a week is about as long as you should ever go between them. Similarly, there are tasks listed as monthly maintenance that your fish will benefit from on a more frequent basis. For example, if you have a lot of heavy feeding fish, you may need to clean the filter biweekly or even weekly.

Clean the Glass

In most tanks, cleaning algae off the glass once a week will suffice. Let me recommend that unless it bothers you, you clean only the panes that are used for viewing—usually just the front glass. Algae, when confined to the glass, is not a bad thing. Algae use up dissolved nutrients and provide fresh food for your fish, many of which will enjoy nibbling both on the algae itself and on the microscopic creatures that live among the algae.

Various scrapers are available for this task, some with metal or plastic blades, some with abrasive pads. If you have an acrylic tank, you must be especially careful to use the proper tools in the proper way to avoid scratching the plastic, but even a glass tank can be scratched. If using a pad, be certain you do not trap any grains

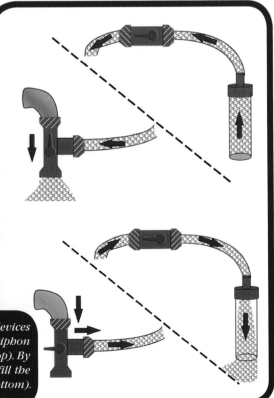

Some water changing devices utilize a water driven pump to siphon water from the tank (top). By closing the pump, you can refill the tank through the same hose (bottom).

of gravel under the pad; as you push them across the glass, they can dig deep grooves.

Vacuum the Gravel

Even if you are changing water every day, you may not take the time to thoroughly vacuum the gravel each time. In most tanks, a good vacuuming once a week will keep the gravel free of detritus. This provides a double benefit: the material removed is no longer in the tank, decomposing and adding to the bioload, and the gravel is stirred and lightly scrubbed, making sure that anaerobic pockets do not form, and that the biofiltration colonies in the gravel are kept viable. Without regular abrasion, the gravel grains can become coated with scale, reducing the surface area for bacterial colonies.

How do you vacuum gravel? Use a siphon with a gravel tube on the end. Much larger than the diameter of the siphon tubing, this rigid plastic tube exerts less suction than the tubing alone does. After the siphon is started, plunge the gravel tube into the substrate. The gravel is lifted partway up the tube, and as it is lifted and agitated, dirt particles are sucked with the water up into the tubing and out of the tank, while the clean gravel falls back to the bottom of the aquarium.

The reduced suction also helps prevent fish from being sucked into the tubing, as even very small fish can usually escape back out of the gravel tube with its reduced current. At the

very least, it slows things down so you have time to stop the siphon and release the wayward fish.

By moving the gravel tube around the tank, you can clean the entire gravel bed. Uneaten food, fish feces, and any other detritus is pulled from the gravel and sent down the drain.

Monthly Maintenance

The following procedures should be performed at least monthly.

Clean the Filter

Mechanical filter media can be washed or replaced with new cartridges. Biomedia must, by definition, be "dirty," that is full of bacteria, to work. They can, however, get clogged with debris, which prevents the flow of water through the medium. A gentle rinsing is usually sufficient to clean them. Make sure to use water from the aquarium at its normal temperature for this rinsing; a large difference in temperature can kill the bacteria, as can the chlorine in tap water.

Many filters use the same medium for mechanical and biological filtration. Polyester pads and foam sponges work well in both capacities. Obviously, if you replace all the filter medium in such a case, you will remove the biofilter. If there are two cartridges side by side, you can

Power Caution

Make sure that any electrical equipment associated with your aquarium is plugged into a GFCI-protected circuit. This could save your life or the life of a family member.

replace only one. The next time, replace the other one. An even better system is to have two cartridges, one in front of the other. The medium through which the water from the aquarium passes first will function as a mechanical filter, trapping all the suspended material. This will leave the second medium to function as a biofilter. At each cleaning, the first cartridge can be replaced, while the second is merely rinsed, if necessary.

Clean the Cover Glass
Full hoods have a strip of glass under the light, and, of course, glass aquarium tops are all glass. This glass will get dusty on the room side, but on the aquarium side it can be obscured with calcium deposits from evaporated water spray and overgrown with algae (especially right under the light).

These can seriously hinder the amount of light reaching the tank and should be removed regularly— especially if you're keeping live plants in the aquarium. If you find you need a scraper to remove these accumulations, you might want to clean the top glass more often.

When You Go Away

Many people fret about their aquarium when they are away from home. Don't. Fish can go two weeks without being fed with no problem. You can feed them well for a week or two before you leave, but do NOT feed them heavily within two days of your departure. Instead, do a big water change to remove the extra wastes from the heavy feeding. Then, while you are gone, do not have someone feed them; it's much more dangerous for your fish than fasting is.

Canister filters allow the hobbyist to tuck their filter away from sight. However, out of sight should not mean out of mind—be sure to check on your canister filter's performance on a daily basis.

Check All Connections

A monthly check of all tubes, tubing, and electrical wires will reveal most problems before they start. Very often before a tube pops off it will start seeping water. A drip is a lot easier to deal with than a flood.

Make sure all electrical plugs are fully inserted and that there are no frayed or wet wires anywhere in the system.

Other Maintenance

Believe it or not, that's about it. Many aquariums have been running for a decade or more with just these simple maintenance procedures. Without a doubt, keeping the gravel clean and the water changed will cover most of your tank's needs—and keep your fish thriving for many years.

Chapter 5

Feeling Good

Aquarium fish are generally hardy creatures with strong immune systems, and it is not uncommon for aquarists to have little or no trouble with sick fish. There are, however, certain ailments that can occur, and it is important to know how to recognize and treat them.

That said, more healthy fish are harmed by indiscriminate medicating than sick fish are saved. Many people have the idea that there is an appropriate medication for every ailment.

Often when a medication does not seem to improve their fish's condition, these people will treat them with another, and another, until there are enough chemicals in the water to make the healthiest fish turn belly up.

It simply is not necessary to be constantly dumping drugs into your aquarium to keep your fish healthy. Maintaining the proper conditions for your fish will in almost all cases keep them from getting sick, and providing the proper conditions will usually cure them if they fall ill. Most experienced aquarists have very little experience with fish illness. They go years without their fish getting sick.

There are fish illnesses which are very serious that are usually found in freshly caught or imported specimens. Fortunately, these are rare because unfortunately, they are not easily treated. Often one of the first symptoms is death. On the other hand, commonly occurring problems can be effectively treated, so those are what we will take a look at here.

Hypochondria

It is important not to become a hypochondriac about your fish. In the same way that medical students studying pathology are often convinced that their headaches, muscle strains, or queasy stomachs are, in fact, symptoms of some grave and obscure disease, fish owners frequently read about all sorts of ailments their fish can conceivably suffer and begin to interpret every irregular move or slight difference in appearance as evidence of some dire affliction.

In both cases, people aren't being stupid, they are just letting their imaginations run too freely. Many diseases have very similar symptoms, but it is not a good idea to assume that a rare, exotic disease is the problem when symptoms first appear. In fact, I'll go so far as to recommend that you do *not* read about fish diseases.

Teaching Respect for Living Things

Trying to keep fish healthy teaches a child that all living things can suffer, and that we should do everything we can to alleviate their suffering. Children have an innate concern for other creatures, and a home aquarium can help them develop this attribute.

The more exotic diseases of
fish are difficult to diagnose and are
not likely to be curable. They are also
extremely unlikely in your aquarium.
In this chapter we'll cover the most
common medical problems and how
to deal with them. For anything
more, you will need to consult
an expert.

Injuries

Fish can be injured by rough handling,
sharp objects in the tank, or fin-
nipping tankmates. Cuts and bruises
are for them much as they are for us:
minor injuries that will heal quickly
unless they get infected.

You cannot slap a bandage on a
fish, but keeping the water clean with
frequent water changes will lower
the bacteria count, and a teaspoon of

salt per gallon will help by increasing
the fish's slime coat to protect the
wound. Basically, you want to keep an
eye on the injury until it is healed, but
nothing needs to be done unless it
develops signs of infection.

The fins of a fish show remarkable
powers of regeneration. Even if the fin
is bitten off right to the base, it will
most likely grow back completely. All
that is needed is time, but if the fish
is having trouble swimming because
of the lost fin, it should be moved to
a tank of its own until it is swimming
normally again and can fend for itself
in a community.

Illnesses

How do you know if a fish is sick?
The best way is to know what your
fish look and act like when they are

First, almost all medications have a negative effect on biofiltration bacteria, ranging from decreasing the colonies to wiping them all out completely. This means you will have to cycle the tank again. In addition, many medications kill plants, so if you have live plants, they may not survive the treatment if you treat sick fish in your main tank.

Finally, the presence of gravel, ornaments, plants, and detritus can complicate treatment. Some medications are inactivated by organic matter or absorbed by substrates, making it difficult to gauge dosages. Also, fish pathogens that have a life cycle that includes a free-swimming

Eye injuries often lead to blindness.

well. If you do, then a sudden negative change in a fish's appearance or behavior can be indicative of disease. By a negative change I mean things like listlessness, loss of color, clamped fins, or spots on the body. Even these depend on your knowledge of the healthy fish, though. Consider the clown loach, which becomes pale when dominant, while most other fish get brighter colors. Or the betta, which normally rests on the bottom with fins closed, which in other fishes is often a sign of illness.

Is a Fish Sick, or Is the Tank Sick?

If only one fish is showing symptoms, it is best to remove that fish and treat it in a separate tank. You should keep an eye on the rest of the tank, in case more fish succumb. It is often a good idea to remove the affected fish, even if all of them are sick, for several reasons.

£4.25

Sick fish often cower in the corners of the aquarium and exhibit clamped fins.

stage often hide, while in a bare hospital tank they are easily siphoned out with daily water changes.

Diagnosis & Treatment

While the absolute diagnosis of any fish disease requires microscopic examination or even necropsy, the most common can often be correctly identified by close observation. Sometimes bringing a bright light over to the tank can help in determining what the problem is. Another option is to net out the affected fish, put it in a glass jar, and hold it up to a light source for close inspection.

A fish infected with ich looks as if it's been salted.

You must realize, however, that without lab tests, you *cannot* have a definite idea of what is wrong with your fish, or if anything really is. If, for no other reason, not really knowing what may be wrong with your fish is cause enough for you to be very careful in medicating your fish. It is also the reason that many experienced aquarists take the first step of isolating the fish in question, stepping up the temperature a bit, and beginning an aggressive water-change regimen. No matter what is wrong, a little warmth and a lot of super-clean water will help, and very often it is all an out-of-sorts fish needs to perk right up.

Ich

Ich or ick, named for the parasite that causes it, *Ichthyophthirius multifiliis*, is probably the only fish ailment you can easily identify and treat. Make no mistake, this is a potentially deadly disease with a possible mortality rate of 100 percent, but if caught immediately, the survival rate can also be 100 percent. Some fish are much more prone to this affliction than others, but any species of fish can succumb to it. You must treat all of the fish, as the disease is highly contagious.

I mentioned that it is caused by a parasite—a protozoan that has a varied life cycle. It is the nature of the life cycle that enables us to effectively combat this parasite, so it is important to understand the organism's basic biology.

The diagnostic symptom of ich is the presence of the parasites embedded in the fish's skin. They appear as little white bumps, giving the fish the appearance of having

An ich parasite magnified 100 times.

been salted. It is important to remember that these parasites also embed themselves in the fish's gills as well as on the skin and fins.

Inside each nodule is a single parasite that constantly scrapes against the fish's tissue, eating the resultant body fluids and pieces of flesh. It is clear by the affected fish's behavior that the infection is extremely uncomfortable.

When the parasite is mature, it breaks out of the nodule, drops from the fish, and attaches to a surface, where it begins to divide. Within its capsule it makes hundreds—even up to 1,000—copies of itself. These then break free and swim around, looking for a host. They have about 48 hours to find a host before they die. When they find one, they burrow into the fish's skin and begin the cycle over again.

People are often amazed by the speed with which this disease can take over a tank. If one becomes hundreds, then the next generation is hundreds of hundreds! In no time at all there is a massive infestation.

The only time that the parasites are susceptible to treatments is when they are free swimming. The rest of the time they are encapsulated and protected from chemicals.

The speed of the life cycle depends on temperature and can be greater than a month. At tropical aquarium temperatures, it is less than a week. This is why the first course of treatment is to raise the temperature of the water. At about 80°F (27°C) the life cycle takes only a couple of days. This means that a new batch of free swimming parasites will hatch out every two days, and they can be killed at this point.

How can they be killed? Well, temperature is one way. A temperature of 90°F (32°C) will kill the free swimming parasites. Most tropical fish can tolerate this temperature for the week to 10 days it will take to completely wipe out the ich infestation. Remember, though, that water this hot has a very limited capability of carrying dissolved oxygen, so increase the water flow dramatically. Ich compromises a fish's gills, increasing its need for oxygen even more.

Salt can be used to kill the parasites. There are also several chemical preparations that are effective. You can purchase these at your aquarium retailer, and you should follow the label instructions carefully, especially as to dosage. Remember that a single treatment cannot eliminate ich, since by the time the next batch of parasites hatches out, the medication will be degraded.

No matter what treatment you select, you should vacuum the tank bottom at least once a day. This removes a great many of the incubating parasites before they can hatch out their free swimming offspring.

In fact, ich can be successfully treated simply by moving the fish to a new bare tank every 12 hours. This keeps the fish ahead of the parasite's life cycle. They drop off the fish and begin dividing, but before they hatch out, the fish are moved. Once all the embedded parasites have dropped off the fish, and in the absence of any new free swimming parasites,

Ulcers like this one may respond to treatment with salt.

the disease is cured.

What about the original tank? Well, if you are treating all the fish in another aquarium, by the time they are cured, the parasites in the home aquarium should have all hatched out and starved to death, especially if you increased the temperature in that tank as well as in the hospital tank. I say "should have" because there is some evidence that the ich pathogen can at times enter a resting state and survive without a host for a while.

If possible, keep the fish in the hospital tank for a couple weeks to make sure, and keep a close eye on the fish after you return them for any sign of reinfection.

The Expert Knows

Salt

Salt remains one of the best treatments for fish ailments. Most freshwater fish can tolerate some salt in their water, but most fish pathogens cannot. Salt also increases a fish's slime coat, helping to ward off parasites like ich. If you are unsure as to the amount of salt you should use to treat any one ailment, be sure to contact your local veterinarian or aquatic health care professional.

Fungus

Fungus is one other common ailment that can usually be correctly diagnosed. Fungus infections are often secondary, following other injuries or infections. Injured fins and lips are commonly attacked by fungus. The fungus appears as a cottony white growth. The affected fish should be moved to a bare container for treatment,

Many fish illnesses are contagious and may infect all the inhabitants within the tank.

which can consist of any of a number of medications made specifically for this problem. Fungus is not normally contagious, but the other fish in the tank should be watched for any signs of it.

Prevention & Quarantine

The best way to treat all fish ailments is with prevention and quarantine. The very best investment you can make in your fish's health is to have a quarantine tank for any new fish

Quarantine & Hospital

The best investment you can make in your fish's health is a spare tank to be used for quarantine and as a hospital tank. It need not be large or fancy. A bare-bottom aquarium with a heater and a simple air-driven sponge filter is perfect.

purchases. The same aquarium can be used as a hospital tank when you have ill fish.

The most fervent proponents of quarantine are usually aquarists who have experienced the tragedy of adding a new (often inexpensive) fish to a tank only to lose their entire collection of cherished and expensive fish to some ailment the newcomer brought with it.

By quarantining all new fish for two to four weeks, you give any pathogens time to manifest themselves. You can then treat the fish, but if the treatment is unsuccessful, at least the only fish that dies is the new one, not your whole collection.

Quarantine is also for the new fish's benefit, however. After all the handling and transport to get to your retailer and then to your home, a fish can be pretty beat up and worn out. It also has been exposed to lots of other fish and lots of other pathogens, and it will be weak. Trying to establish itself in a tank where everyone already has his own territory, while also trying to adjust to new water conditions, may be too much for it to bear.

Chapter 6

The World of
Fishes

When you go to choose a pet puppy or kitten,
there may be dozens of breeds to choose from,
but there's only one species of dog and one of cat.
When you want to stock an aquarium, there are
thousands of species to choose from! In fact, there
are more than 20,000 species of fish in the world,
and at least a couple thousand that are commonly
available in the hobby.

With so many species, it is not surprising that fishes are a diverse group. There are fish in the Arctic and in hot springs. The smallest vertebrate is a fish (less than half an inch), and there are fish large enough to swallow a human whole. Fish are found in oceans, rivers, lakes, streams, ponds, springs, and even temporary pools and puddles.

Your local retailer probably has an enormous variety of fish in stock and can special order many more species. If you've never kept fish, however, it can be quite daunting to see tank after tank, each filled with a different species. How can you choose?

In this chapter, we'll look at the major types of fishes, and at some examples of commonly available

species that will work well for your first tank community.

Killies & Livebearers

Killifish and livebearers make up a group known as cyprinodonts.

Swordtails are popular livebearers.

While killifish are not commonly available in regular retail aquarium stores, livebearers are in many ways the backbone of the trade. There are many species of livebearers, and many different groups of fishes have species that give birth to live young rather than laying eggs, but in the hobby, the term "livebearer" usually refers to poeciliids, the ever-available guppies, mollies, platies, and swordtails.

The males have a modified anal fin, called a gonopodium, which is used to transfer sperm into the female's vent. Technically, these fish are ovoviviparous, which means

20,000 Choices

There are so many fishes that it is impossible to cover more than a handful of them in this book. You should consult other books to learn about other possible specimens for your aquarium.

that the fertilized eggs are retained within the female's body, but the fry develop off the yolk, without any direct nourishment from the female. It is not even necessary to purchase a male to get fry. Female livebearers can be inseminated at very young ages, and they can store viable sperm giving birth to litter after litter without further matings.

Many beginning aquarists are surprised when their red platies have blue babies. Since a female livebearer can store sperm, the only way to get offspring of the same variety as the parents is to buy the adults from unmixed tanks and to keep only one variety per tank.

These fish lure many people into a lifelong aquarium hobby, as within a couple weeks after they are added to a tank, there are usually fry—tiny copies of the adults. An extremely lucky hobbyist will get to witness their birth, dropping from their mother, only animating before they hit the ground and swim away.

All are available in a staggering variety of body types, fin lengths, and color patterns. Many of these different strains were created from hybrids between closely related species and by careful selective breeding.

If properly cared for, a female livebearer will drop a litter about once a month. The

number of fry can be as a few as a dozen for young, small females, or as high as 150 for large, fully mature females. The babies will instinctively seek cover—the best is floating plants, living or plastic. This is important even if you choose to remove the pregnant female to her own tank, as often the mother will eat her own fry.

While you may raise a few young to maturity in a community tank, the best growth is in special rearing tanks, or even outdoor ponds like fish farmers often use. Plenty of food and daily water changes will produce comparable results, since the idea is to maximize nutrition while minimizing pollution.

Feeding livebearers is no problem, as they will eagerly consume all types of foods. All of them should have some vegetable matter in the diet, so a spirulina algae flake is good to include. You will often see your livebearers picking algae off the glass and other objects in the tank.

Guppies

Once dubbed the "missionary fish" because of all the people it converted to the aquarium hobby, today the guppy is more often found in the tanks of specialized breeders than in the tanks of beginners. Several factors have contributed to this shift, including one or more diseases at fish farms that caused this once "cast-iron" fish to become unreliable. Healthy stock, however, is available. Your dealer should be able to special order some for you, unless they keep them in stock.

A variatus platy.

people's fancy over the decades.

Keep in mind that guppy breeding is very different from having some guppies reproduce in your tank. To preserve the qualities of a given line requires several tanks dedicated to the strain and careful selection and culling. As with all color-bred livebearers, any young produced in a community tank will probably be quite different from their parents.

Mollies

Despite their availability, mollies are not the best choice for a new aquarist. They are wonderful fish, but they are not as hardy or as adaptable as the other livebearers. To properly maintain them, you have to pay more attention to water chemistry, accommodations, diet, and temperature than you do with other species.

Specifically, they require either hard, basic water or brackish

The Endler's livebearer has been steadily gaining popularity. This is an isolated guppy population that, given many more centuries, might become a separate species. Old aquarists who remember the original Trinidad guppy find Endlers to be extremely similar.

Some hobbyists who want "wild type" guppies purchase feeder guppies and work with them. Such fish are often in poor shape, and may harbor disease or parasites, but with a little attention they can often be cleaned up and used as the foundation for a breeding population.

Of course, the fancy guppies of the show circuit are magnificent examples both of guppies' genetic variability and of guppy breeders' skill. Underneath all the elaborate finnage and designer colors are the same hardy and hearty fish that have captured so many

A sailfin molly.

conditions. Many wild mollies are found in pure seawater. They also are extremely sensitive to dissolved metabolic wastes, and they need large tanks with frequent water changes. A single pair of mollies might be all right by themselves in a 20-gallon (76-l) tank, but only with plenty of water changes, and a larger aquarium would be better; if you want to keep other fish with them, a 50-gallon (189-l) tank is about the minimum. Although all livebearers appreciate vegetable foods like algae, mollies seem to require more. Last, mollies do best at the upper end of normal tropical aquarium temperatures—near 80°F (27°C).

A blue platy.

You will see mollies kept in lesser conditions than these, but if you ever get to see properly maintained mollies, you will notice a big difference! It is a shame to condemn these beautiful fish to accommodations which are so stressful for them, especially when there are so many other fishes that will thrive in conditions that mollies find barely tolerable.

By crossing various species of wild mollies and by careful selective breeding, fish farmers have produced mollies in a color palette that ranges from pure white to pitch black, from solid to piebald to spotted, from light orange to deep red. Sailfin mollies are especially attractive—a 5-inch (13-cm) male displaying to a female is a sight to behold.

Platies

Platies may be the ideal first fish. Hardy, lively, and peaceful, they are available in just about any color or combination. They get along well with each other and with other fishes.

The foundation for domesticated platies was mainly the various color morphs of two species: *Xiphophorus maculatus* and *Xiphophorus variatus*. From these, dozens of different strains have been developed. In addition, swordtails and platies were often crossed. The presence of heavy-bodied swordtails with small swords is a reminder of the mixed background of these fish.

Most wild platies are silvery blue or orange, but domesticated strains can have a base color of white, yellow, gold, orange, red, blue, or black. Wagtail platies have a solid body with black fins; this is especially striking in red wagtail platies. Some platies have black dots across their bodies; when the base color is white, these are called salt and pepper platies. There are many other varieties as well.

Swordtails

The foundation for domesticated swordtails was mainly the various color morphs of one species: *Xiphophorus hellerii*, though most likely there were other species hybridized into them as well. In addition, as I mentioned, some color varieties were transferred to swordtails from platy strains, and vice versa. Such mixed heritage is sometimes visible in the form of rudimentary swords on platy-like fish, or reduced swords on swordtail-like fish.

These cousins of platies are also excellent choices for your aquarium. The only drawback they have is that the males can be quite aggressive to each other, and they require larger tanks than platies, due to both their greater size and their aggressiveness. You should keep only one male per tank (unless the tank is very large—100 gallons [378 l] or more), and it is best to have at least two or three females so that he does not excessively harass any particular one.

The male has a sword-like extension at the bottom of its tail fin. It uses this sword in displays meant to impress females

or to intimidate other males. Wild swordtails are green with iridescent stripes and sometimes black markings. Domesticated strains are available in all the colors and combinations of platies, plus a few more.

Tetras, etc.

The characids are another very popular group in the hobby, and they include tetras, pencilfish, and several other common fishes, of which tetras are certainly the most widely available. Although tetras are often thought of as small, peaceful, brightly colored fish, there is enormous variety in the group, and there are drab species as well as large, predatory ones. The common tetras in the hobby, however, are perfect for peaceful community aquariums. There are many nice African tetras, but most of the species at your retail store are likely to be from the New World.

South American tetras are always a favorite!

All tetras are schooling fish, and schooling is important for their well-being. These fish, being small and brightly colored, are instinctively very skittish, always on the lookout for predators; when they are not in a school, they become neurotic and are constantly stressed by perceiving themselves in a dangerous environment. This leads to early death.

This is not just bad for them; you will not get to see the fish's natural behaviors if there are just one or two of them in the tank.

Different species school more or less tightly, ranging from a bunch of fish each moving around in the general vicinity of the others to a tightly choreographed school that moves as one. In fact, the same fish can school in different ways at different times. When they feel secure, they may drift apart, but if startled, all the fish will immediately seek the safety and comfort of the group.

Visual cues that fish use to school include, among other things, color, pattern, and ornaments such as iridescent stripes, ocellated spots, and fin movements. Fish with similar cues will often school together, so you can find more than one species in a school.

Healthy tetras may spawn in your aquarium, but it is unlikely you will get any fry, since the eggs and the newborns are delicacies to all the fish, including the parents. With enough cover, and without overly predacious tankmates, some may survive, but don't count on it. Nevertheless, spawning will mean a good show for you as the fish put on their best colors and display to each other.

Tetras will eat all live, frozen, freeze-dried, and dried foods. They are especially fond of small live foods like daphnia or bloodworms. There are many species of tetras suitable for a first community aquarium. We'll take a look at some of the most popular and

SMALL FRY

Fish as Pets

Children often think of fish more like a pet cat or dog, while their parents regard them more as ornaments. Children often name each fish, and they can become quite attached to them individually.

widely available species, but keep in mind that there are many more.

Neon Tetra & Cardinal Tetra

These fish are quite similar and will often school together. The red on the neon tetra does not extend all the way across the body, while on the cardinal tetra it does. The highly iridescent blue stripe gives the neon its name, and the cardinal also has it. These fish require special conditions for breeding, but they will adapt to almost any

water supply in a community tank. They especially appreciate a planted tank with similarly small and peaceful fishes.

Many aquarists make the mistake of putting small neon tetras into a community tank with larger fish. There is something about these fish that advertises them as delicious tidbits. Probably the bright colors of the fish, which aquarists appreciate so much, also grab the attention of other fish. In any case, the neons will be snapped up by any fish able to get their mouth around them. They will also be snatched by many fish unable to swallow them, often with the death of the neons being the result. I have seen fish barely larger than neons try to ingest the neons. To avoid this

problem, you should put neons into a tank and allow them to grow for a few weeks before adding the other fish. When they are larger, they are less of a temptation, and the fact that they aren't being added to the tank by the big two-legged creature who always brings dinner helps as well.

Black Neon Tetra

The black neon tetra is in many ways a black and white version of the neon, but it is much more beautiful than that description indicates. The thick black stripe and the thin iridescent blue-white stripe create a subtle beauty that complements more colorful tetras well.

Lemon Tetra

This fish is a transparent yellow with black edges on the unpaired fins and a bright lemon yellow streak on the anal fin. This understated coloration is highlighted by an intense red on the upper half of the eye. The lemon tetra is a quiet and

peaceful fish, and a school of them will often hang about, just looking beautiful.

Black Tetra

Black tetras are larger fish, reaching about 2.5 inches (6 cm). With its unique body shape and black and white markings, this fish is instantly recognizable. An all-white variety has been developed, and unfortunately, it is often dyed to make "mixed-berry tetras" of various colors. There are so many beautiful tetras that it makes no sense to strip fish of their slime coats with acid and dip them in dyes!

Glowlight Tetra

While many fish have blue or green iridescences, this tetra has a bold, body-length, neon-red stripe. It gets just over an inch (2.5 cm) and is completely peaceful.

Bloodfin Tetra

More elongate than many tetras, the bloodfin is a shiny silver fish with—you guessed it—red fins. One of the hardiest and longest-lived tetras, a school of these 2-inch (5-cm) fish will brighten any tank.

Pristella

This beautiful little tetra is silver with black and white ornaments on its fins and a pale red tail. When it swims, it flicks its dorsal and anal fins in a manner reminiscent of the schooling tail motions of the scissortail rasbora; I have had the two species school together in my tanks, and I'm certain it is the similarity of this visual cue that united these South American tetras and Asian rasboras.

71

Serpae Tetra

There are several very similar species of tetra that are called serpaes. They are peaceful and make excellent community inhabitants. They are overall red, with more intense red in the fins. Black on the dorsal and anal fins combines with a black shoulder spot as contrasts.

Bleeding Heart Tetra

This tetra somewhat resembles a giant serpae tetra. The common name comes from the red spot on the fish's chest.

At 2.5 inches (6 cm), this is a robust tetra, and while it cannot stand up to aggressive fishes, it will bully much smaller tetras.

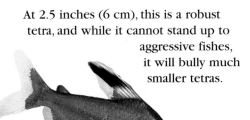

Barbs, Danios & Loaches

The term "barb" covers a great diversity of cyprinid fish in Africa and Asia. The goldfish could be considered a barb but usually is not. Many of the smaller species of barbs are popular aquarium fish (large barbs can reach several feet in length!). Danios are cyprinids from Asia that are in many ways similar to tetras. Loaches are Asian species that are mostly adapted for life on the bottom, much like native suckers.

Tiger Barb

The brightly marked orange and black tiger barb with its red fins makes a stunning display in a large group. Although sometimes a fin nipper in small groups, the fish in a school of 8 or more is usually so busy chasing each other that they leave other fish alone, but don't tempt them with long-finned tankmates.

Foolproof Fishes

Everyone has different experiences, but most aquarists agree that danios, platies, barbs, and white clouds are extremely hardy and adaptable, and they make great choices for your first tank.

This species comes in several domesticated color morphs, including albino and moss green, but the wild coloration is extremely hard to beat! They are hardy and long-lived, and they will eat any type of food.

Gold Barb

This fish is a brilliant gold, with a few black splotches. Another hardy and long-lived species, the gold barb is a wonderful community specimen. Again, they may be a bit nippy, but in a large school they should get along fine.

Cherry Barb

As hardy as the first two barbs, the cherry barb is also extremely peaceful and unlikely to nip fins. If you put a school of them into your tank, the males will soon assume a velvety maroon coloration, and they will display constantly to the females, which are quite pretty in shades of brown and beige. An albino strain has also been developed.

Rosy Barb

This is another barb in which the males take on a red coloration. Also, a few domesticated strains have been developed with increased color. The metallic silver on both sexes makes an impressive display, but these fish do get fairly large—almost 6 inches (15 cm)—so a big tank is necessary for a school of them.

Zebra Danio

It is hard to think of a fish as hardy, as lively, or as peaceful as the zebra danio. The wild type has blue and silver stripes along its whole body. There are also gold and albino strains, as well as long-finned varieties. Personally, I find long fins distasteful on fish as energetic and streamlined as these. The normal fish are color in motion, but the long-finned version has to struggle to swim and can never cavort like its unmodified cousins.

Scissortail Rasbora

There are many rasboras in the hobby, many of them smaller and more colorful than this fish. This species, however, is particularly hardy, while some of the smaller rasboras are much fussier about water conditions. When this fish swims, it jerks the top and the bottom of its forked tail toward each other in a scissoring motion. The scissortail is a long-lived, peaceful, and active schooling fish that will liven up an aquarium large enough to accommodate its eventual size of 5 inches (13 cm).

White Cloud

The white cloud or White Cloud Mountain minnow is an old favorite. It can tolerate room temperatures and does not require a heated tank. It is one of the most adaptable and hardiest fishes available. Placed in a tank by themselves, they will multiply, as they rarely eat their eggs or fry. This species is extinct in the wild, but it survives in the hobby as a

perennially popular aquarium specimen, totally peaceful, hardy, and beautiful. The iridescent green stripe juveniles is even brighter than that of a neon tetra.

Red Tail Shark

Actually a loach, this fish is striking, with a solid black body and a bright red tail. It used to be much more popular than it is now. That is probably because so many aquarists discovered the downsides of this fish.

First, you can only reasonably maintain one loach per tank, as loaches fight among themselves. Second, the fish does not stay small, but grows to at least 5 inches (13 cm). Last, when it matures, it becomes extremely territorial and may claim the entire tank as its territory. When this happens, it will attack any other fish in the tank.

Clown Loach

The clown loach is extremely popular. Its bright colors and appealing personality are real assets. It is generally peaceful, though it should not be kept with shy, retiring species, which may be intimidated by the loaches' frenetic pace. These fish should be kept in schools for their own benefit as well as yours. Some of the behaviors you will witness from a school are audible clicking noises that the fish make when squabbling over territory or food—loud enough to be heard across the room from the aquarium.

This fish has several negatives. It grows to a foot (30 cm) in length and fades in color as it grows. Unlike many fish, however, it grows rather slowly, and it will take several years for it to reach this size. It is quite sensitive when first brought home, and many succumb in the first week or so, often to ich. Unfortunately, it is also sensitive to many medications. The best way to handle a clown loach with ich is to raise the temperature to 90°F (27°C) and maintain this temperature for 10 days.

This fish has the perverse habit of playing dead. Many a heartbroken aquarist has gone to net out a corpse—only to have it dart off when the net approaches.

Yo-Yo Loach

This is an even better choice than the clown loach. It is not as colorful, but it has a very interesting brown-on-tan pattern. The name comes from the fact that on many specimens, the pattern on the side can be seen as including the letters "YOYO."

This fish is peaceful, enjoys being in a group of at least five, and stays small for a loach—about 4 inches (10 cm). Like all loaches, it is most active at night, but it doesn't disappear during the day, and it will always be one of the first to get to the food. It spends most of its time either chasing its schoolmates around the tank or poking into every nook and cranny for overlooked tidbits.

Labyrinth Fishes

These Asian fishes have a special labyrinth organ, which functions like a supplemental lung. Many of them live in stagnant water, which is often low in oxygen. This organ permits them to breathe air to obtain oxygen to supplement what they are able to extract from the water through their gills. These fish make periodic trips to the surface for a breath of air.

Many of these fish also utilize air during spawning. The males make nests of bubbles. Depending on the species, the nests can be quite elaborate and incorporate pieces of plants. The fertilized eggs are placed inside bubbles and stored safely in the nest. The male guards the nest and blows any eggs that fall out back into the bubbles. Other species are mouthbrooders, and the male keeps the eggs in his mouth until they hatch.

Betta or Siamese Fighting Fish

Although most bettas are males kept in small bowls or vases, this fish is a beautiful addition to a peaceful aquarium. This only works, however, provided the tank is not too deep, has very mild water movement, and does not contain any energetic, curious, or nippy fishes.

Two males will rip each other to shreds, but a male betta will not attack other species. Female bettas, which lack the long fins and full colors of the males, will usually get along with each other. You can keep a male with one or more females, as long as the tank is large enough for the females to get away from the male in the event that he is ready to spawn and they are not.

Blue or Three-Spot Gourami

A long-time favorite in the hobby, the blue gourami's only liability is its eventual size of 6 inches (15 cm). The domesticated strains include, besides the original blue with two black spots (the eye making a third spot), opaline, gold, and platinum. All of them are the same species.

Pearl Gourami

Smaller and a bit more delicate is the pearl gourami, named for the white spots all over its body. The background color on a healthy male ready to spawn can assume a violet cast, making this an extremely beautiful fish. This fish is a bit more delicate than the blue gourami, but it is also even more peaceful. Like all gourami, it uses its long, thread-like pelvic fins like

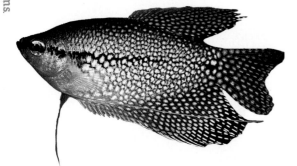

whiskers, feeling its way through underwater obstacles.

Dwarf Gourami

The dwarf gourami has iridescent silver females and red and blue-barred males. Several color varieties have been produced, but they are usually available only as males, as the females are held back by the breeders. This is a very peaceful fish.

Catfish

With a few thousand species worldwide, there are catfish of all sizes and types, from miniscule parasitic species to 15- feet (5-m) monsters that are among the few fish known to swallow human beings. There are omnivorous scavengers, meat-eating predators, algae-eating herbivores—even catfish that eat wood. Most catfish live in fresh water, but there are marine and brackish species, too. Almost all of the popular aquarium catfish, however, belong to two families: the armored catfish of South America and the sucker-mouth catfish of Central and South America. A few others are available, but some are not suitable for the home aquarium.

Cory Cats

There are more than 100 species of "cory" catfishes, but only a handful of them have been constant favorites in the hobby for many years. The green or bronze cory cat is available just about everywhere, as is an albino form. These fish are comical and lively, and they are most happy when they are in a group. The group can be made up of different species of cories, as they almost all get along very well.

Cories are unusual in that they utilize atmospheric air to supplement their gills. You will often see one make a beeline for the surface, grab a mouthful of air, and return to the bottom. They actually swallow the bubble of air, and they are able to extract oxygen from it in the digestive tract.

Pleco

The name "pleco" is short for "plecostomus," a former genus name that was originally applied to almost any loricariid catfish. Today the common pleco is known to be in the genus *Hypostomus*, but the name has stuck. It is also widely applied to bristlenose cats of the genus *Ancistrus*, which are better choices for your tank than the regular plecos.

Plecos get big—almost 2 feet (60 cm) long—and are quite territorial. Bristlenose cats, on the other hand, stay under 6 inches (15 cm) and are extremely peaceful. They are also excellent algae eaters. You will not often see the fish, as they are shy and nocturnal, but every morning you will see their handiwork: algae rasped away from the glass and from objects in the tank.

Upside Down Cat

The upside down cat is adapted for life belly-up. It loves to hide under a floating object—belly up, of course—and to dart out when it detects food. These fish are happiest in a school of six or so and peacefully mind their own business. You will probably never see them right side up.

Cichlids

Most cichlids are not suitable for your community tank. However, with more than 2,000 species of cichlids in Asia, Africa, and the Americas,

there are at least a few that you can consider adding to it.

Traits shared by a great many cichlids which make them unsuitable for most community tanks include: large size, aggressive natures, digging propensity, and territoriality when spawning. Dwarf cichlids eliminate the first concern. Since many dwarf cichlids are also peaceful, that leaves many species under consideration. Many of these are cave spawners, so much of their excavation is under a rock or a piece of driftwood, meaning they are less likely to leave you with a crater-pocked aquarium with all the plants uprooted. They still defend their brood, but many of them are content with very small territories, and although they keep other fish away, they don't commandeer 90 percent of the tank space the way their larger cousins do.

"Dwarf" is a relative term, however, and some small cichlid species are not usually considered dwarf cichlids precisely because they do not fit the general description just given and are thought of instead as simply smaller versions of regular cichlids. On the other hand, there are some cichlids that get fairly large, but are

Size Myths

Myths abound in this hobby about how big fish grow, about how they will not outgrow a tank, and about how large a tank you need for a fish of a specific size. The truth is—any aquarium that prevents a fish from growing is a torture chamber. To figure the minimum-sized aquarium you need for a specific fish, take the adult length of the fish into account. The depth of the tank, measured front to back, must be several inches greater, than the length of the fish (so it can turn around easily), and the length of the tank, measured end to end, must be several times that of the fish (so the fish can swim without immediately hitting the end).

unusually peaceful, and these *are* usually called dwarf cichlids. One of these is the krib.

Kribs

Kribs are true old-timers in the hobby. They are suitable for communities in larger tanks. The female is typically more colorful than the male, especially as they get ready to spawn, when the female develops an intense red belly.

These fish will not bother other fish in the tank unless they have spawned, in which case the parents will keep all the other fish away from their babies. They are good at this, but depending on what other fish you have, they may not be able to protect them forever.

of room. If you have an aquarium of 40 gallons (150 l) or more, you can include an angelfish or two.

The original wild angelfish is a silver fish with black bars, but they have been bred in numerous domesticated strains with various fin lengths and a great many colors and patterns. No matter what strain you have, they are all the same species and need identical care.

Angelfish

Angelfish are not considered dwarf cichlids, but they are quite mild mannered, and they have unusually small mouths for a cichlid. This makes them suitable for large community aquariums with good-sized tankmates. A common mistake is to include baby angelfish in tanks that are too small. They grow quickly and need plenty

Chapter 7

Getting Along

One of the greatest frustrations novice aquarists face is when their fish do not get along. This can range from one fish dominating another through various aggressive behaviors all the way to one fish killing all its tankmates. Now that we've had an overview of the various fish that are available, let's look at how to avoid problems when combining them.

Choosing Compatible Tankmates

There are various ways in which fish can fail to get along, and they generally stem from a combination of factors. Thus, two fish that should not be kept together might very well be suitable for an aquarium with a different selection of tankmates.

Big Mouths

Many fish are active predators, and some will even tear large fish to pieces, while other fish are peaceful plant eaters that never hunt other fish. No fish, however, will pass up a worm or a bug, small enough to swallow. It is safe to assume that any fish will eat any other fish that is small enough to fit into its mouth.

An oscar's open mouth is often the last thing a small fish sees.

A Quick Point to Consider

Not all of the fishes mentioned in this chapter have been covered in the previous chapter. If you have any question as to whether or not the fishes you plan on housing together will live peacefully with each other it is suggested that you consult your local aquarium shop, an Internet forum, or another printed source.

It is easy to underestimate the size of a fish's mouth. There are some fish that can swallow fish as large as themselves, which may seem baffling. Many fish have extendable mouthparts that create a much larger opening than is indicated by the outline of the closed mouth.

It is the size of the mouth, not the size of the fish that matters. A 3-inch (7.5-cm) swordtail will live peaceably with a 1-inch (2.5-cm) guppy, but many a 3-inch (7.5-cm) goby or catfish would simply swallow the guppy—and maybe even the swordtail! To be safe, make sure the smallest fish in your tank is considerably larger than the largest mouth. Remember to take adult sizes into account; often a fish grows a lot and suddenly is big enough to swallow its tankmates.

Color is Only One Feature

The bright colors of tropical fish draw people's attention immediately, but remember that there are many other attributes, including behavioral ones, by which you should choose the fish for your aquarium.

Conflicting Habits

Incompatibility can be a simple matter of two fishes' behaviors being at odds: keeping a clown loach and a pleco in the same tank, for example. In such a case, either of these fish would be fine in your tank, but not both together. Each fish likes to set up a territory centered on a cave or crevice; they will fight for the best spot in the tank. In a very large tank with many hiding spots, they may each set up their own separate territory, but in most tanks it's best to keep only one of the fish.

Another example is keeping fast and slow feeders together. Kuhli loaches are nocturnal, shy, slow feeding, bottom dwellers. If kept with most common fishes, who eat up all the food you put in before it hits the bottom, they will starve to death. One way around this problem is to feed a wafer of food after you turn off the lights at night. It will sink to the bottom and the loaches can feed leisurely on it while their tankmates sleep.

Another common mismatch is keeping livebearers and angelfish together. The adults can get along fine, but you are unlikely ever to see any livebearer fry. In the wild, angelfish prowl through aquatic vegetation, patiently hunting down any small animal moving among the plants. Once they see potential prey, they are relentless in tracking it down and consuming it. In a regular community tank with floating plants, many livebearer fry will survive, but in tanks with angelfish in them, probably none will.

The classic bad grouping is of three of the most popular fish:

Dwarf cichlids can be territorial.

angelfish, neon tetras, and tiger barbs. All three are wonderful fish, and any of them can work well in your first aquarium. Together, however, they are a very bad combination. First of all, neon tetras are colorful bonbons to an angelfish. Neons barely reach an inch (2.5 cm), but that little angelfish will quickly grow into a fish six times or more as large, and will then be perfectly capable of swallowing the tetra. On the other hand, tiger barbs find the long, flowing fins of an angelfish irresistible to nip. Although their nipping is more playful than malicious, the result is the same: shredded fins. The new aquarist just sees two marvelously colored fishes and one stately and graceful species, but there are really two combinations: a predator with a bright tiny fish, and a delicately finned fish with a playful and sharp-toothed tease.

Tiger barbs are notorious fin nippers, especially when not kept in schools of six or more.

Here's another example. Yo-yo loaches, cory cats, and kuhli loaches all are good choices for a community, and they are all bottom feeders with nocturnal tendencies. You cannot, however, keep kuhli loaches with either of the others because they will starve to death. The yo-yos or the cories will get all of the food before the kuhlis even know it's there. Keeping yo-yo loaches with catfish is perfectly acceptable, since they are roughly equal in assertiveness and will compete well for the food.

Goldfish are not recommended for tropical community tanks.

SMALL FRY

Explaining Fish Compatibility

If your child is old enough to participate in picking out the fish for your aquarium, make sure that he or she understands that certain fish do not get along well, and that you may have to reject a particular request because of this.

Fish to Avoid

You might think that if a fish is for sale at your local store, it is a good potential specimen for your aquarium. Unfortunately, several species that are extremely popular and widely available are not suitable for your first community aquarium. Some of them may be perfectly suitable for other types of tanks, and others should not be kept by anyone who does not have an aquarium comparable to the size of a public aquarium.

Fortunately, responsible dealers won't stock completely inappropriate species, but they will certainly stock fishes with specialized needs for the benefit of their customers who have the knowledge and equipment to house them.

Let's take a look at commonly available fish that you should steer away from when stocking your first tank.

Getting Along

Most cichlids are a bad choice for community tanks.

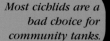

Goldfish

Goldfish have been popular pets for centuries, and breeding these beautiful animals goes back way before there even was an aquarium hobby. Goldfish, however, are never appropriate in a tropical fish community.

The biggest reason for this is that they aren't tropical fish. Goldfish prefer much cooler water temperatures and are stressed at tropical ones. Overly warm water also speeds up their metabolism, making them produce even more waste than they normally do.

Goldfish grow too big for the typical home aquarium. Oh, I know people do keep them in a bowl, but they shouldn't. Goldfish grow 1 to 2 feet (30 to 60 cm) long. Even much smaller specimens need a minimum of 10 to 20 gallons (37 to 75 l) per fish at cool temperatures—even more at tropical temperatures.

If goldfish appeal to you, great! Set up a goldfish tank. An unheated 55-gallon (210 l) aquarium with three or four nice specimens can be a beautiful display. But don't mix goldfish with tropicals.

Cichlids

The cichlid family is a very large group of fishes, and they are extremely popular. Many aquarists specialize in cichlids and have large fishrooms filled with tank after tank displaying just different cichlids. There are inch-long (2.5-cm) cichlids and 3-feet (90-cm) ones, but one of the most appealing characteristics of this group is the often extended parental care that they display. In all, they are beautiful and fascinating fishes.

Unfortunately, however, almost all cichlids are not suitable for your aquarium. Many are too large or too territorial, but even those that are not present problems. Some require special conditions, either in water chemistry or in temperature, while others have hard-to-meet dietary requirements. A great many cichlids are too aggressive for a

A cute baby oscar quickly grows into a gigantic fish.

communities tank, and some cannot even be kept in a community with other cichlids.

There are a few exceptions, (the community-safe cichlids discussed in the last chapter), but as a general rule, if a fish is a cichlid, it will not work in your tank. When in doubt, leave the cichlid out.

Juveniles of Large Species
Many juvenile fish make great aquarium specimens, but they grow too large for the home fish tank. The cute little babies give no indication that they will soon grow to become larger than most dogs. If you care for your fish properly, these species will outgrow your tank quite quickly— usually eating all of your other fish on the way. You cannot count on finding a home for your pet once it grows; after all, it will probably be too big for just about anyone else's aquarium, too!

The 5 Worst Fish for Your Tank

The following fish, some of which are quite commonly available, should never be put into your tank:
1. **Iridescent shark:** grows to 4 feet (1.2 m).
2. **Chinese algae eater:** too big, too nasty.
3. **Pacu:** some species of these piranha look-alikes grow to 4 feet (1.2 m) long.
4. **Colombian shark cat:** grows large, needs salt water as an adult.
5. **Redtail cat:** grows to be bigger than most breeds of dogs.

In addition, many lose their appealing attributes as they grow. Consider the Chinese highfin banded shark or loach. Usually sold at around 3 inches (7.5 cm) long, this fish has alternating dark and light brown bars and a greatly elongated dorsal fin. It is sold as a peaceful community fish, which it is—for a short while. The adult fish is 2 to 3 feet long (60 to 90 cm); as it grows, its unusual high-bodied shape shifts into a slender cylindrical shape, and its pattern disappears, becoming a muddy brown coloration. Turning from beautiful duckling into ugly swan, such fish are, unfortunately, fairly common.

A great many large catfish, some of which could properly be labeled gigantic, are sold as juveniles:

• The intriguing 2-inch (5-cm) redtailed catfish practically begs you to take it home, but this is a voracious predator that can top 5 feet (150 cm) in length.

• The so-called iridescent shark is a very delicate, large-growing and very nervous, schooling catfish that cannot be properly housed even in most public aquariums. It has no place in the home aquarium.

• The Columbian shark cat is the juvenile of a marine catfish that grows more than a foot long (30 cm) and cannot live its entire life in fresh water.

• The channel catfish, available in both normal blue and albino forms and widely sold as juveniles, is a 4- to 5- feet (120- to 150-cm) monster predator totally unsuitable for the home aquarium.

It is best to avoid any fishes called "eels."

It's a Fish-Eat-Fish World

Even a peaceful, herbivorous fish will eat another fish that is small enough to swallow. Make sure that your smallest fish is considerably larger than the largest mouth in the tank.

Chinese Algae Eaters

These fish are widely sold to combat algae. Unfortunately, they are a bad choice. It is true that they eat algae when small, but soon they grow very large—to 12 inches (30 cm)—and become very territorial, even downright nasty. There are many other fish that are much better at eating algae without terrorizing their tankmates.

Fish Called Sharks

There are no freshwater sharks that are suitable for the home aquarium. Many fish are called "sharks" because of a perceived resemblance to the shape of those cartilaginous predators, but they are typically loaches or catfish. Most of these fish are not very suitable for your first tank, and a few, as you have seen earlier in this chapter, are completely unsuitable. As a general rule, avoid anything called a "shark."

Fish Called Eels

True eels are not for your aquarium. Unfortunately, neither are most fish that are called "eels" because of their general shape. The only group that holds any promise is the so-called spiny eels. These fish, however, are best reserved for after you have some experience. Most of them are way too large, and the few smaller species have husbandry requirements that differ from most community fishes.

Bad Cousins of Good Community Fish

You might be fooled into thinking some fish would be good for your aquarium because many of their close relatives are. For example, the tinfoil barb is often available. This is a flashy silver fish with red fins, and a school of them is an awesome sight. The problem with them is simply that they grow way too large for an aquarium of less than 100 or 150 gallons (400 to 600 l). Usually sold as small juveniles, they quickly grow to 14 inches (35 cm).

Similarly, you might be reassured that a "bucktooth tetra" would be a good choice, especially if you were told it only reaches about 3 inches (7.5 cm). This fish, however, has sharp teeth and the temperament of a piranha (to which they are closely related). Put a few of these into your tank, and they will shred every other fish in there.

90

The 5 Best Fish for a New Community Tank

1. Cherry barb
2. White cloud
3. Cory cat
4. Platy
5. Bloodfin tetra

This is why it is extremely important that you research any fish you wish to purchase *before* you bring it home. Knowing its size and its family is not enough; you must find out what the specific characteristics and needs of the fish in question are.

Fish Labeled "Freshwater"

You are certainly aware that there are marine or saltwater fishes and freshwater

fishes. In this book we are concerned only with freshwater species. There are, however, other fish, called brackish fishes. These live in habitats in which fresh water and ocean water mix, like river mouths, mangrove swamps, and estuaries. Very often the juveniles are brackish, but the adults live out in the sea.

Several marine fish have brackish cousins, and these are often labeled as freshwater versions of the marine species. Thus you will see names like "freshwater moray eel," "freshwater stonefish," "freshwater flounder," etc. In virtually every case, however, these are not freshwater species, although they will live for a little while in water with no salt in it. Soon, though, they will succumb unless they are maintained in a brackish or marine aquarium.

Territoriality

Although there are a handful of exceptions, almost all fish that maintain territories do so on the tank bottom. They typically use visual reference points to define their territories—rocks, driftwood, plants, etc. Often a cave or hole is the focal point of the territory, with an area around the opening being defended as well.

Territoriality in itself does not make a fish unsuitable for your tank. If you have only one territorial fish, and if it only maintains a small territory around its lair, things may work out fine.

Some fish, like some of the dwarf cichlids and some catfish, are only

The Expert Knows

Multilevel Stocking

To get maximum enjoyment from your aquarium, you should choose fish from all three zones: those that stay near the surface (hatchetfish), those that spend most of their time in midwater (tetras, livebearers, barbs), and those that prowl the substrate at the bottom of the tank (loaches, catfish). Of course, during feeding times, be sure that all the fishes get their fare share of the food!

aggressive when spawning, and only then toward fish that threaten their eggs or fry by coming too close. These fish do nicely in a community tank—at least until they spawn. If you only keep one specimen, that is generally not a problem; however, sometimes a lone individual will come into spawning readiness and still defend a territory while waiting for a mate to hopefully arrive.

Stocking & Overstocking

The most common compatibility issue is overcrowding—all of the fish chosen are good choices, but there are just too many of them. The recommendations above do not leave room for additions, and they are all made with the assumption that you will be using adequate filtration and making a minimum 50 percent water change at least once a week. With

maintenance like that, these groupings should work out fine.

To come up with your own fish stocking schemes, use the ones given here as a guide. You can substitute similar size fish of similar temperament anywhere in the groupings with a good possibility of success. Body mass that determines how much bioload a fish puts on a system. A 3-inch (7.5-cm) kuhli loach less than the thickness of a pencil is nowhere near the mass of a swordtail the same size.

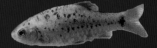

Fish Selection for Aquariums Up to 20 Gallons (76 liters) in Volume

What are good fishes for your first aquarium? You can see by looking at these charts that just a basic listing of fishes is not entirely a good way to determine which species you should and should not house together. Let's first look at a few samples that provide a basic community for aquariums up to 20 gallons (76 liters) in volume.

A Real Mix

	5 gal.	10 gal.	15 gal.	20 gal.
Platies	2	3	3	4
Zebra Danios	3	5	5	7
Cherry Barbs	2	2	3	3
Cory Cats	1	3	3	4

Another Mix

	5 gal.	10 gal.	15 gal.	20 gal.
Gold Barbs	2	3	3	4
White Clouds	3	5	6	8
Swordtails	2	2	3	4

All Tetras

	5 gal.	10 gal.	15 gal.	20 gal.
Lemon Tetras	2	3	3	4
Bloodfins	3	3	4	5
Glowlights	3	4	5	6
Serpae Tetras	0	3	3	5

All Asian Fishes

	5 gal.	10 gal.	15 gal.	20 gal.
Dwarf Gourami	0	1 pair	1 pair	1 pair
White Clouds	4	6	6	8
Gold Barbs	2	3	3	5
Cherry Barbs	2	3	3	5
Yo-Yo Loach	0	1	2	2

Fish Selection for Aquariums from 29 gallons (76 liters) to 55 gallons (210 liters) in Volume

Now let's consider some similar selections for aquariums up to 55 gallons (210 liters) in volume. The same mixes could go in the less-common 50-gallon (190-l) aquarium, which measures 36 inches (91 cm) by 18 inches (46 cm) by 18 inches (46 cm). Either of these aquariums will make a substantial display, and they are large enough to house a similar number of fishes.

A Real Mix

	29 gal.	45 gal.	55 gal.
Platies	3	5	6
Zebra Danios	8	10	12
Serpae Tetras	6	6	10
Lemon Tetras	6	6	10
Cory Cats	3	3	5

Another Mix

	29 gal.	45 gal.	55 gal.
Blood Fins	2	3	3
Black Neons	3	5	5
Glowlights	2	3	3
Cherry Barbs	3	3	3
Bleeding Hearts	4	6	8

A Big Mix

	29 gal.	45 gal.	55 gal.
Swordtails Only 1 Male	5	5	6
Tiger Barbs	5	6	8
Yo-Yo Loaches	2	3	5
Bleeding Hearts	4	6	8
Blue Gouramis	2	2	3

All Tetras

	29 gal.	45 gal.	55 gal.
Serpae Tetras	6	6	10
Black Neons	8	10	12
Lemon Tetras	6	8	10
Bleeding Hearts	4	6	8
Glowlights	8	10	12

All Asian Fish

	29 gal.	45 gal.	55 gal.
White Clouds	12	12	15
Yo-Yo Loach	3	3	4
Gold Barbs	6	8	10
Blue Gourami	2	3	3

All Neons/ Cardinals

29 gal.	45 gal.	55 gal.
24	30	36

All Angelic Setup

	29 gal.	45 gal.	55 gal.
Angelfish	4	6	7
Cory Cats	5	7	8

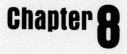

Beyond the

Tank

Chances are good that if you succeed with your first aquarium, you might become even more interested in tropical fish and wish to move on to the next stage. What that stage may be is up to you. Some long-term aquarists never have more than one tank, though they occasionally upgrade to a larger one with different species. Most often, however, once you are bitten by the bug, you start looking for places to put just one more tank.

Cichlids, like this firemouth, provide extended parental care to their young.

The artistic type of aquarist maintains several aquascaped tanks, each as beautiful as the next. Then there are pragmatic hobbyists who have tier upon tier of utilitarian tanks for breeding various species. Probably the most common type of intermediate or advanced aquarist is the one who has several show tanks, which are often community tanks, as well as a fishroom of plainer setups for breeding and growing out fry.

Even the direction that aquarists take as they grow in the hobby can differ. Some continue to expand their hobby to include more and different fishes. Others find one or two groups of fishes that fascinate them, and they specialize in just those groups. In any case, there are three major areas into which aquarists typically expand.

Breeding

Very often fish breed in a community aquarium, and whether or not any fry survive, the aquarist is often hooked on watching the miracle of life unfold. The second aquarium setup for many hobbyists is a breeding tank.

The number and diversity of breeding strategies used by fishes is astounding. There are fish like the cod that broadcast several million miniscule eggs to the waves, and others that nurture a half dozen large eggs in their throat until they hatch, then watch over their fry.

Other fish inject their eggs into crevices in rocks, or lay them inside living clams, or parasitize other species' nests like cuckoos. Some fish give birth to live young, and some of those provide nourishment for their developing fetuses much the way mammals do.

Some breeding fish form monogamous pairs, some have harems of several females to one male, and some have females that mate with several males. There are group spawners, and there are even fish that have three or more sexes. The sex of some fish is determined genetically, while others become male or female depending on the water parameters while their eggs are developing. Yet other fish begin life as one sex and later turn into the other sex—some species start out as females, others begin as males.

Add to all this the fact that many fish have breathtakingly beautiful breeding colorations and many exotic spawning behaviors, including heartwarming parental care of the young, and you can see why so many people get interested in fish breeding.

People Don't Breed Fish; Fish Breed Fish

99

Although we speak in the shorthand of breeding our fish, we realize that it's the fish that spawn; we just provide the proper conditions to get them to spawn. For many people, that is the appeal. Fish that are not kept in the best condition do not usually breed, so a successful spawning is a feather in the aquarist's cap—a confirmation of his or her skill in maintaining and conditioning fish.

There are some species that are very easy to induce to spawn, like the legendary zebra danios that can spawn in the plastic bag on the way home from the pet shop. There are other species that have never been spawned in captivity, despite many attempts to encourage them to produce offspring. Between these two extremes are fairly easy and moderately difficult species to match anyone's level of skill and patience at having their fish reproduce.

SMALL FRY

A Lifetime Hobby

When children get involved with tropical fish, they often become lifetime aquarists. Teens and young adults may take time off for schooling, but they usually return once they start a family.

The zebra danio is an extremely easy-to-breed egglayer.

Sometimes when one or two people succeed with a species, they discover the important stimulus conditions and report a procedure that works for everyone from then on. Occasionally, however, the initial successes appear to be flukes; even the people who had the success are unable to eplicate it, even with the same pair of fish!

Then there are fish like the extremely popular neon tetra. The conditions necessary to breed this species were discovered decades ago, but they are so painstaking that very few aquarists bother. These fish spawn in the Amazon in such huge numbers that no amount of harvest and export diminishes the overall population, so almost no one takes on the challenge of breeding them.

Beginning fish breeders, however, usually want more of a sure thing, and they choose one or more of the species that spawn quite readily in an aquarium. There are plenty of these, both livebearers and egglayers.

False Stereotypes

The breeding strategies of the most common aquarium species are often overgeneralized. The livebearers, guppies, platies, and swordtails, usually reproduce for every aquarist who keeps them. Egglaying species like tetras and barbs breed less readily for most aquarists. This often leads to the false conclusion that livebearers are very easy to breed, but egglayers are hard.

The fact is that there are many livebearing tropical fishes that are extremely difficult to get to breed successfully in a home aquarium, some of them are very closely related to those common breeds that just happen to breed easily for everyone. There are also egglaying species that seem to breed under just about any conditions.

In other words, whether you want to work with very easy, easy, moderate, hard, or almost-impossible species, and whether you want to work with livebearers or egglayers, there are fishes that are perfect for you.

Propagation vs. Selective Breeding

Unlike most other pet breeding, fish breeding has two major components. The first is propagation, and this is what is lacking in most pet breeding. People do not usually breed cats or dogs just to get more. They work with a specific breed, using the finest examples with the goal of improving the breed. Pet-quality animals are usually neutered, and only show-quality animals are reserved as breeders.

With tropical fish, however, propagation is often important. First of all, whenever possible, aquarists like to purchase captive-bred animals. These have the threefold benefit of being hardier, adapting easily to new conditions, and making no impact on natural ecosystems. In addition, however, there are many fish whose existence in the wild is precarious at best, and captive propagation may be the only hope for the future of these species. In fact, there are fish species that are extinct—except in aquarists' tanks.

Zebra plecos are an extremely difficult-to-breed egglayer.

Sharing the Passion

Conventions of national fish clubs provide a way for large numbers of aquarists to have fun, learn more about their hobby, and share their passion for fish.

The other type of breeding, selective breeding, also has a place in the tropical fish world. Livebearers, cichlids, barbs, and tetras are among many fish that have domesticated strains, with new ones being developed all the time. These strains are the equivalent of cat and dog breeds, and the same principles apply. Only the best show-quality stock is used as foundation, and the offspring are carefully culled and picked over so that the strain is maintained and even improved with each generation.

Many of the most popular strains over the years were produced by aquarists with home hatcheries—basement breeding operations with an extremely limited scope. This is because the necessary

contributions to such projects are dedication, observation, and extreme patience. A hobby breeder can invest these, while commercial operations need to worry about the bottom line of profit, not creative experimentation.

Clubs

The next step for many new aquarists is to join an aquarium society. Local clubs exist all over the country, with regional, national, and international organizations for many specialties. These groups provide a wealth of opportunities for their members.

Educational Opportunity

Typically, speakers give presentations at monthly club meetings. Sometimes one of the members simply gives an address on some aspect of the hobby, and sometimes an expert is invited to come and address the group. Many "ordinary," nonprofessional

Selective breeding has produced many fancy livebearers.

Join a Club!

The best way to grow in the aquarium hobby is to join an aquarium society. There is sure to be one near you. Ask your local aquarium retailer, or search online to find the closest one.

speakers are quite entertaining as well as informative. An informal, fun-loving atmosphere is the norm for aquarium clubs. Just belonging to a club also provides plenty of information. The combined knowledge and experience of the members of some groups is overwhelming, and fellow members can tap this vast information storehouse any time they need it.

Fish & Supplies

Clubs often have sales or auctions, as well as classified ads in their monthly newsletters and maybe fish and equipment listings on a bulletin board, real or electronic. Fish, plants, live foods, and equipment are among the usual items traded and sold. In addition, members often swap fish informally, and visits to other people's fishrooms often result in a few bags being carried home.

Many fish species are not available commercially, and one of the only ways to obtain them is from members of a club. Several specialties exist in which almost all fish are obtained in this way, or from importers. Cichlid, catfish, and killifish fans often cannot find what they are looking for in regular aquarium shops. On occasion some very rare fish become distributed in

the hobby simply because a club member from somewhere around the country imported or even collected the particular fish species in the wild and then made some available to members of various clubs.

Motivation & Inspiration

Humans are both gregarious and competitive, and the impetus to do something can come from seeing it done by our peers. The automatic water-changing system one club member designs and installs might stimulate another club member to make an even better one. Everyone can benefit from the exchange of ideas.

And what about burnout? We all reach a point when doing the same thing gets old, and we need new ideas. Sometimes a monthly speaker or a surprise on the auction table is enough to jump-start us, and we become freshly energized about the hobby.

Fellowship

We can't leave out the friendship and fellowship that are the hallmarks of aquarium clubs. It is always nice to have the opportunity to meet and associate with people with similar interests to ours. This is especially true for people who are quite

The Expert Knows

The Allure of Spawning Fishes

Part of the fascination aquarists have for breeding fish is the incredible diversity of reproductive behaviors. You could breed a different species every week of the year and still not observe two that spawned in the same way. Some species of fishes are easier to breed than others. Hobbyists wishing to breed their fish should start out with easier-to-breed species and work their way up to the harder ones.

104

Freshwater Aquariums

passionate about something like tropical fish.

Aquarists normally learn not to say too much about their hobby, either for fear of ridicule or because they get tired of explaining the same thing over and over. At a club meeting, everyone is equally ridiculous about fish and eager to share a common knowledge of them.

Many long-term friendships are first forged in clubs, and many groups have joint undertakings such as fishroom tours and even going on collecting expeditions in the tropics together. An occasional marriage of two club members has even been documented!

Because local associations often have ties to neighboring clubs, the sphere of contacts can be quite large, and the network of friends can extend

quite a distance. When you add in associations of associations, or national clubs, the network grows enormously. In fact, the aquarium hobby really knows no borders. It is especially strong in the Americas, Europe, and Asia, giving aquarists a truly worldwide influence. It is not uncommon for aquarists from different continents to meet and to stay in touch, all because of aquarium societies and their events.

Shows & Conventions

Club membership often leads aquarists to national and international shows and conventions, although many of the attendees at these events are not members of a local aquarium club. Typically the conventions feature three or more days of presentations, workshops, and panel discussions, punctuated with plenty of fun-filled activities, socializing, and fish sales. Many aquarists bring their families along, and there are scheduled activities for the non-aquarist members of the families as well.

In effect, these conventions are mega-scale club meetings. The same benefits accrue, only on a national and international level.

Speakers

Speakers from around the world come together to give the latest news, updates on scientific matters, and reports of collecting expeditions. Often there are so many speakers that two or three sessions run simultaneously.

In addition, many national clubs are actively involved in conservation,

You will often see less common species at a fish show.

and they often have fundraising events that finance both conservation and scientific research. These feed back into the organization, and, in turn, educate the members.

There are many opportunities at these conventions to speak one-on-one with some of the most prominent experts in the field, and to get answers to your questions and suggestions for your fishroom.

Fish & Supplies

The big clubs have big auctions. In addition, many attendees sell fish, both in sales rooms sponsored by the event and privately. Some of the rarest fish in the world can be found only at these big national sales.

Resources

Magazines

Tropical Fish Hobbyist
1 T.F.H. Plaza
3rd & Union Avenues
Neptune City, NJ 07753
Phone: (732) 988-8400
E-mail: info@tfh.com
www.tfhmagazine.com

Internet Resources

A World of Fish
www.aworldoffish.com

Aquarium Hobbyist
www.aquariumhobbyist.com

Cichlid Forum
www.cichlid-forum.com

Discus Page Holland
www.dph.nl

FINS: The Fish Information Service
http://fins.actwin.com

Fish Geeks
www.fishgeeks.com

Fish Index
www.fishindex.com

MyFishTank.Net
www.myfishtank.net

Planet Catfish
www.planetcatfish.com

Tropical Resources
www.tropicalresources.net

Water Wolves
http://forums.waterwolves.com

Associations & Societies

American Cichlid Association
Claudia Dickinson, Membership
Coordinator
P.O. Box 5078
Montauk, NY 11954
Phone: (631) 668-5125
E-mail: IvyRose@optonline.net
www.cichlid.org

American Killifish Association
Catherine Carney, Secretary
12723 Airport Road
Mt. Vernon, OH 43050
E-mail: schmidtcarney@ecr.net
www.aka.org

American Livebearer Association
Timothy Brady, Membership Chairman
5 Zerbe Street
Cressona, PA 17929-1513
Phone: (570) 385-0573
http://livebearers.org

Association of Aquarists
David Davis, Membership Secretary
2 Telephone Road
Portsmouth, Hants, England
PO4 0AY
Phone: 01705 798686

British Killifish Association
Adrian Burge, Publicity Officer
E-mail: adjan@wym.u-net.com
www.bka.org.uk

Canadian Association of
Aquarium Clubs
Miecia Burden, Membership
Coordinator
142 Stonehenge Pl.
Kitchener, Ontario, Canada
N2N 2M7
Phone: (517) 745-1452
E-mail: mbburden@look.ca
www.caoac.on.ca

Canadian Killifish Association
Chris Sinclair, Membership
1251 Bray Court
Mississauga, Ontario, Canada L5J 354
Phone: (905) 471-8681
E-mail: cka@rogers.com
www.cka.org

Federation of American Aquarium
Societies
Jane Benes, Secretary
923 Wadsworth Street
Syracuse, NY 13208-2419
Phone: (513) 894-7289
E-mail: jbenes01@yahoo.com
www.gcca.net/faas

Goldfish Society of America
P.O. Box 551373
Fort Lauderdale, FL 33355
E-mail: info@goldfishsociety.org
www.goldfishsociety.org

International Betta Congress
Steve Van Camp, Secretary
923 Wadsworth St.
Syracuse, NY 13208
Phone: (315) 454-4792
E-mail: bettacongress@yahoo.com
www.ibcbettas.com

International Fancy Guppy Association
Rick Grigsby, Secretary
3552 West Lily Garden Lane
South Jordan, Utah 84095
Phone: (801) 694-7425
E-mail: genx632@yahoo.com
www.ifga.org

National Aquarium in Baltimore
501 E. Pratt Street
Baltimore, MD 21202
(410) 576-3800 (daily 9:00 a.m. to
4:30 p.m.)
www.aqua.org

Index

Bold numbers indicate illustrations.

Dedication
To my parents, who innocently bought me my first fish.

About the Author
David E. Boruchowitz has been keeping and raising fishes for more than 50 years. The author of numerous books and articles, he also serves as Editor-in-Chief of *Tropical Fish Hobbyist* Magazine. David's scientific training and many years of writing for aquarists enable him to bring order to the sometimes chaotic world of aquarium keeping. David lives on a farm in New York State with his family and over a dozen aquariums.

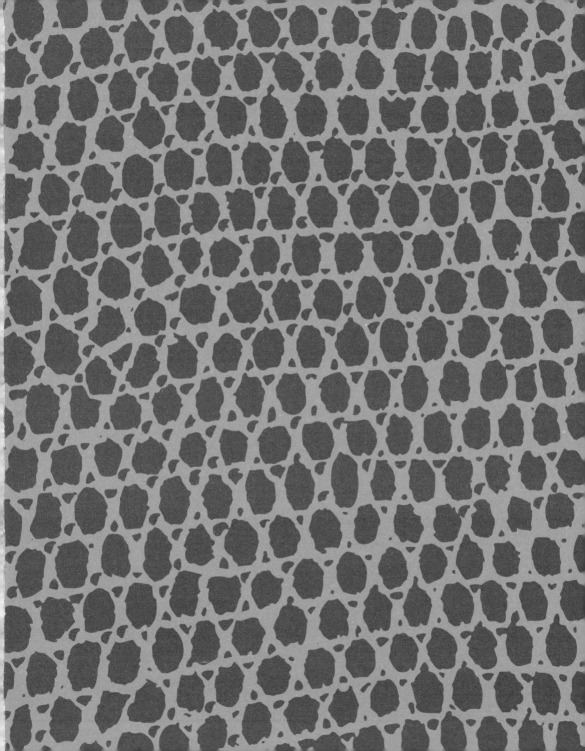

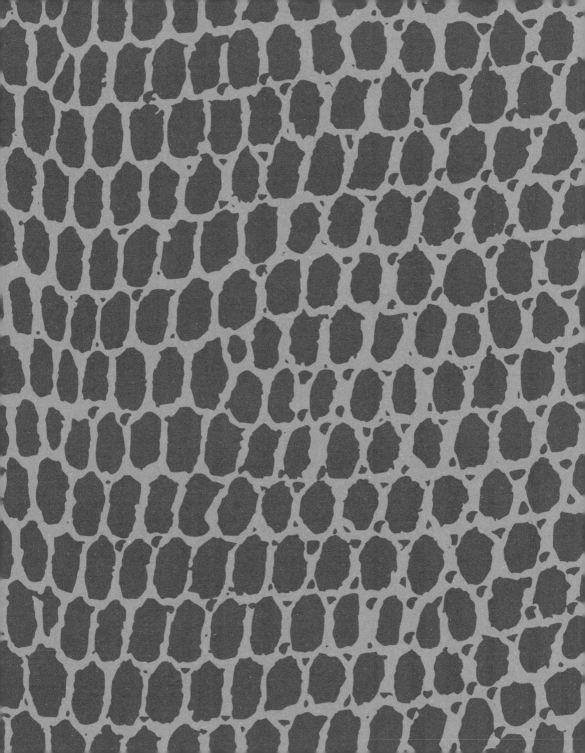